Curtin's Gift

Curtin's Gift

Reinterpreting Australia's greatest Prime Minister

JOHN EDWARDS

ALLEN&UNWIN

This project has been assisted by the Commonwealth Government through the Australia Council, its arts funding and advisory board.

First published in 2005

Allen & Unwin
83 Alexander Street
Crows Nest NSW 2065
Australia
Phone: (61 2) 8425 0100
Fax: (61 2) 9906 2218
Email: info@allenandunwin.com
Web: www.allenandunwin.com

National Library of Australia
Cataloguing-in-Publication entry:

Edwards, John K.
    Curtin's gift : reinterpreting Australia's greatest Prime Minister.

Includes index.

ISBN 1 86508 704 1.

1. Curtin, John, 1885–1945. 2. Prime ministers—Australia—Biography. 3. Politicians—Australia—Biography. 4. Australia—Politics and government—1901–1945. I. Title.

994.04092

Frontispiece: *John Curtin crossing the street* (n.d) JCPML 00376/55 (Records of the Curtin family)
Set in 10.5/15.4 pt Galliard by Bookhouse, Sydney
Printed by McPherson's Printing Group, Maryborough

10 9 8 7 6 5 4 3 2 1

For Deborah, Alex and Harry

Contents

Acknowledgments

Australians cherish the memory of Prime Minister John Curtin, mostly for the wrong reasons. He did not save Australia from invasion by Japan, he did not create the alliance with the United States, and the single decision for which is he most revered—the return of Australian troops from the Middle East—was not what we now remember it as. But he did create the foundations of the modern Australian Commonwealth, a magnificent achievement which reflected three decades of thoughtful reading and debate, and for which he is rarely credited. I argued this first in a lecture at the John Curtin Prime Ministerial Library (JCPML) in Perth in 2001. The then editorial director of Allen & Unwin, John Iremonger, asked me to develop the idea into a book, and this is the result.

The book owes a lot to John, who not only commissioned it but also made extensive comments on drafts and outlines up to his final illness. Whatever merit it has honours the memory of a fine, selfless man who contributed immeasurably to Australia's intellectual life.

The lecture would not have been given or the book written without the encouragement and interest of the

Archivist of the JCPML, Kandy-Jane Henderson. She invited me to accept a year-long fellowship with the Library, which allowed me to develop the lecture. Concealed behind Kandy-Jane's unobtrusive manner is a will of steel. Whatever crowding claims the rest of my life made on my time, Kandy-Jane's gentle and persistent inquiry made sure there was always a little left for the book. She completely understood the direction in which I was working, often anticipated it with new material, and kept me up to date with other work in the area. Her colleagues Lesley Wallace, David Wylie and Lesley Carman-Brown sustained the flow of material, read and commented upon various drafts, and provided a community of interest in the book. To Kandy-Jane and her colleagues I am deeply grateful.

Throughout, Professor David Black, now Historical Consultant with the JCPML, has been of the utmost help. His own work on Curtin's letters, speeches and bibliography shows that there is a great deal more to say about Curtin and his period than we have yet acknowledged. David first identified to me to me the importance of the early months of 1942 in determining the foundations of the modern Commonwealth, and he was later kind enough to make helpful comments on a draft.

Work on the book was much enriched by access to the papers of former journalist and government adviser Tom Fitzgerald, which were generously made available to the JCPML in 2002 by his son Dennis and other members of the Fitzgerald family. Reading his research some years after I had worked out my own standpoint, it was quite evident that Tom was not only exploring in the same direction, but had gone much further. Tom was working towards a wonderful book.

Much of what is in this book was once well known. The two volumes of the official history of the war economy by S.J. Butlin and C.B. Schedvin are still the foundational accounts of war time economic policy decisions. In recent years scholars have widened and deepened our under-standing of Curtin and his times. Their works include David Day's full-length biography, David Horner's accounts of strategic decision-making, Dick Hall and Clem Lloyd's work on Curtin's press conferences, and JCPML lectures by Peter Edwards and Tim Rowse. Gough Whitlam gave valuable guidance on Curtin's role in education policy.

The Reserve Bank of Australia and the National Archives either provided material directly or guided me to online material upon which many of this book's arguments rest.

After John Iremonger's death from cancer in 2002, Allen & Unwin's Rebecca Kaiser became my publisher. Her advice was always insightful and wise. Emma Cotter oversaw the book's production, and to her and Carson Creagh I owe many improvements. Barry Howarth compiled the index with his customary thoroughness, informed by his deep understanding of the period. My wife Deborah Hope advised and encouraged me thoughout. Whatever errors are left are mine alone.

1

Sleepless Vigil

Walking home from Parliament after midnight in early March 1942, Clerk of the House of Representatives Frank Green encountered Prime Minister John Curtin pacing the grounds of the Lodge. The Prime Minister's official residence was then adjoined by open fields, so Green would probably have walked up from Parliament House through the scrub that then covered Capital Hill. Australia was at war, but Green was able to step into the grounds of the Lodge and walk around until he found Curtin. For Green to see Curtin in the garden it must have been a moonlit night; Japanese carrier planes had already bombed Darwin and a blackout was enforced even as far south as Canberra. Slit trenches had been dug in the bowling green near Parliament House and Canberra residents had already stocked up on groceries to take into the hills should Japanese invaders reach the national capital.

Green's encounter with Curtin was not accidental. Curtin's driver, Ray Tracey, had told him Curtin had not slept for several days and spent each night walking about the grounds of the Lodge. Tracey hinted that as an old friend Green should stop by and encourage the Prime Minister to get some rest.

Curtin was then 57, slightly under six feet and, because he no longer had time for long daily walks, ten pounds over his normal weight. His grey hair was thinning and he wore black-rimmed spectacles. He had been Prime Minister for five months. It was the first time in his life he had held ministerial office, and those five months were surely the most momentous in Australian history. Eight weeks after he had become Prime Minister, Japan attacked the United States Pacific fleet at Pearl Harbor. Australia suddenly found itself living the nightmare that had troubled it for half a century—war with Japan. It was, Curtin solemnly announced, 'the gravest hour in our history'.

At the same time as it attacked Pearl Harbor Japan attacked the Philippines, Guam and Malaya, and pressed south toward the Netherlands East Indies and Australia. Since European settlement Australian war planning had depended on the British fleet controlling the seas, but three days after Pearl Harbor Japanese planes sank the *Prince of Wales* and *Repulse*, two British warships deployed to Singapore to deter a Japanese attack. A little over two months later, Japan had conquered Malaya and invaded Singapore. The defenders had been forced to surrender, sending 17 000 surviving troops of the Australian 8th

Division to prisoner of war camps. The British fleet in the Pacific had been sunk, the US fleet had been badly damaged, the Japanese army was building in Rabaul, the impregnable Singapore Fortress had been captured and now Australia had lost a quarter of its battle-trained soldiers to Japanese prison camps.

With the British preoccupied by Germany, Australia turned to the United States. Eight weeks earlier, on 27 December 1941, Curtin had published his Melbourne *Herald* appeal to the United States, writing that, 'Without any inhibitions of any kind, I make it quite clear that Australia looks to America, free of any pangs as to our traditional links of kinship with the United Kingdom'.

Singapore had fallen on 15 February, a few weeks before Green walked by the Lodge that moonlit evening. Curtin told Australians the capture of Singapore was 'Australia's Dunkirk' and as Dunkirk had preceded the Battle for Britain, so 'the fall of Singapore opens the Battle for Australia'. He believed that, 'He would be a very dull person who could not discard all his preconceived ideas of strategy and war and who does not accept the fall of Singapore as involving a completely new situation'. Because he was directing his remarks now at the United States as much as Australia he allowed himself the colourful claim that 'the frontiers of the United States of America' and 'therefore, in large measure, the fate of the English speaking world' also depended on this forthcoming Battle for Australia. On 27 February the Australian Chiefs of Staff had told Curtin that Japan was 'at liberty to attempt an invasion of Australia if she so desires'. By 5 March Curtin's Cabinet expected a landing around Darwin in early April, and a landing on the east coast by May.

This national crisis of survival was one that at first glance Curtin was woefully unprepared to meet. He had left school at 14. He had never been a minister before he became Prime Minister. In his political career he had been defeated four times in contests for the House of Representatives, and though his party gained seats he himself was very nearly defeated for a fifth time as Opposition Leader in the election of 1940. Before he became Prime Minister he had left Australia only once, briefly. He had been a polemicist, commentator and agitator for three decades. His most demanding management job was as secretary of a small trade union—a job he had left as much through alcoholism as intellectual fatigue. His election as Leader of the Opposition by eleven votes to ten in the depleted Labor caucus of 1935 had astounded many members of the Parliament House press gallery. The party he then led was torn by divisions, with four separate Labor Parties in South Australia and three in New South Wales. With this very modest preparation he had been asked to form a government, after Prime Minister Arthur Fadden lost his majority in the House of Representatives on the night of 3 October 1941. He continued in office only with the support of the independents, who had brought down the preceding Prime Minister. With so little experience of office, so little distinction in his career, so fragile a hold on power, he faced the very real and immediate threat that Japanese armies could land in Australia within weeks.

As Prime Minister Curtin went into his Parliament House office around nine in the morning and did not leave until midnight, it was perhaps well past midnight when Green walked by. Curtin would likely have been outside, smoking a cigarette in the holder he always used. It would have been so much better for his health if he could drink occasionally and not smoke at all, Curtin's daughter later recalled, but 'of course he couldn't'. Curtin was likely still wearing his suit, or perhaps just the high-buttoned vest he preferred that showed very little of his tie. He would have eaten the roast lamb with vegetables he generally had for dinner. His wife Elsie was probably at home at their cottage at the Perth beachside suburb of Cottesloe, but Ray Tracey would have been somewhere around the Lodge. He took care of the ducks and fowls there, and was the Prime Minister's late-night billiards partner as well as his driver. Curtin was perhaps in one of those black moods well remembered by family and friends, which in better times he would walk off in long rambles along Cottesloe Beach or Canberra's Majura Hills and from which his daughter said only his wife or Ray Tracey could reliably cajole him.

Throughout his life and particularly when he became Prime Minister, people responded to what they thought to be his physical frailty. He had a disconcerting cast in his left eye so that people talking to him were not entirely sure where he was looking. Because of it his press secretary

Don Rodgers had great difficulty finding a suitable standard photograph of Curtin—one with 'something like a straight on appearance'—and eventually settled for a side shot. Earlier in his life his alcohol addiction had been serious enough to put him in a private sanatorium. He was troubled with psoriasis, which produced red, scaly and itchy patches on his skin and for which he took a remedy sold as Kruschen Salts. He was depressed for long periods, subject to nervous stomach ailments, and even then he had heart problems. Earlier in the month he had been hospitalised in Sydney for what was said to be 'nervous dyspepsia'. A little over three years later he would be dead of heart disease. These evident weaknesses evoked from both men and women a doting concern for his health, which is what brought Green by the Lodge.

Finding Curtin pacing in the garden of the Lodge, Green gently told him he should get some sleep. Curtin did not answer, and the two men stood in silence for several minutes. 'How can I sleep,' Curtin then asked, 'with our men in the Indian Ocean among enemy submarines?' Sleepless because he had as Prime Minister and for the first time in Australia's history refused in the gravest circumstances a most earnest wartime request of the Prime Minister of the United Kingdom; a request strongly and directly supported by the President of the United States and also strongly supported by former Australian prime ministers and ministers, experienced leaders of the Australian Government who now sat as Opposition members on the Australian Advisory War Council. He had flatly—and repeatedly—refused Churchill's request that leading elements of Australia's 7th Division, then being transported across the Indian Ocean from the Middle East, should be landed in Rangoon to prevent the Japanese from conquering Burma and cutting off a supply line between China and India. Curtin had insisted that the 7th Division come back to Australia, and now the leading troop transport, the *Mount Vernon*, was sailing south. She was an American cargo vessel, so tightly packed with over 4600 Australian troops that the iron bed frames were arranged in rows three deep in the hold and the men spent most of their day lining up for one of the six sittings required for each plentiful but unfamiliar meal of bread, frankfurters and maple syrup. Alone, unescorted, after a voyage that began at Fort Tewfick, Egypt, in early February, the ship now sailed down through the hostile waters of the Indian Ocean to Fremantle.

Green walked with Curtin back up to the kitchen at the Lodge, where he made tea for the Prime Minister. Curtin still refused to sleep, however, and after drinking his tea Green left him once again pacing the grounds of the Lodge. Curtin had every reason to be worried. Japanese forces, now controlled the seas, sky and land north of Australia. By the beginning of March Batavia was being evacuated, Australian and Allied naval ships were evacuating troops and civilians from Sumatra and Java, and the powerful naval forces of Japanese vice-admirals Nagumo and Kondo were hunting south of Java and as far west as the Cocos.

On 1 March, a day that found the *Mount Vernon* 800 miles southwest of Christmas Island, and a convoy of eleven ships with seven naval escorts transporting 10,000 Australians leaving Colombo for Australia, the Japanese navy in the waters north and west of Australia sank the US Navy ships *Edsall* and *Pecos*, then *Pillsbury* and *Asheville*, then the Royal Navy ship *Stronghold*. Australian navy corvettes and minesweepers were fleeing south from the Netherlands East Indies and on 4 March the *Yarra* and its convoy were attacked by three heavy cruisers and two destroyers from Kondo's force. In four days in early March the Japanese navy sank 20 ships in waters north and west of Australia, not very far from where the *Mount Vernon* was or from where many other transports loaded with Australian troops and their equipment would soon pass. Curtin had insisted Australia's battle-trained troops come home, and now they were coming across enemy controlled waters. To Colombo the British relied on their control of the sea and some destroyer escort for the bigger convoys. From Colombo south the faster transports were on their own. Standing on the deck of the *Mount Vernon* as it raced for Fremantle Private Bob Hope, a gunner of the 25th Brigade, looked about for the escorts but saw only the white wake of the ship and empty sea from horizon to horizon.

Curtin's sleepless vigil at the Lodge is surely the most memorable and touching episode in his three years and nine months as Prime Minister of Australia. It was a defining moment in his leadership, not just in the popular perception but also in the sober assessment of history. His insistence on the return of the 6th and 7th Divisions of the Australian Imperial Force from the Middle East would change Australia's relationship with England and the way Australians thought about themselves. In the Australian story the colonies federated into a nation in 1901 and its military forces first won renown fighting on the shores of the Dardanelles in 1915, but it was not until Curtin insisted in February 1942 on the return of its troops to face the imminent threat from Japan that Australia became a truly independent nation.

There is a good deal of truth in this, but the identification of Curtin's place in Australian history with this moment also limits him and our understanding of who he was, what he did and what he means in the Australian story. Part of the Australian tradition of the events of February 1942 is that Curtin was an accidental hero; a reluctant Prime Minister, a man of modest attainments and limited experiences, the poorly educated son of an itinerant policeman and unsuccessful publican, by trade a hardware estimator, a recovering alcoholic, an innocent and an idealist forced by the circumstances of war to compromise lifelong principles—a man who in the words of a newspaper obituary 'had greatness thrust upon him' by war and to which he 'responded greatly'.

It follows that without the war there would not have been very much to Curtin. Historian Stuart Macintyre writes that he would have been 'a mediocre and timid peacetime Prime Minister'. Historian Fred Alexander wrote that Curtin 'in his reputation, in his actual career . . . was indeed a fortunate and even a lucky man' whose 'reputation was greater than his intrinsic qualities'. Curtin is credited with one great episode in Australian history, and dismissed from the rest.

He represents an Australian ideal of an ordinary man who rises to the occasion and the Labor Party ideal of a leader of abiding and radical principle recognising the practicalities of great office. Curtin sometimes liked to present himself in this way. His conservative opponents spoke of him as sincere, reliable and honest, with the hint perhaps that he wanted the subtlety, education, intelligence and breadth to be as interesting and formidable as they were. By contrast we think of his great contemporary and rival for importance in our history, Robert Menzies, as an unusually gifted and urbane barrister, witty and commanding, who far from having greatness thrust upon him rather wanted for a challenge sufficient to his remarkable gifts—a challenge such as being the Dominion's representative in the British War Cabinet, or perhaps Prime Minister of England.

In some accounts of the period Curtin was not only an accidental and reluctant Prime Minister, but even as Prime Minister was responsible for only a narrow—though admittedly vital—part of national leadership. He was Prime Minister and Minister for Defence Co-ordination, but in March 1942 he put Australian military forces under the command of American general Douglas MacArthur. While Curtin took care of the rear it was MacArthur who took care of the front. Nor, in the standard account, did he run much of the rear. The economy was managed by Curtin's friend, Treasurer and successor, Ben Chifley, who according to David Day's biography not only ran the economy in war but also provided the vision for postwar Australia. It is little wonder that Curtin's insistence on the return of the 6th and 7th is so important in his story. After crediting other claims, there is not much else left.

There is another way of thinking about Curtin, however, that places him as the central figure in the creation of modern Australia. He did not become so accidentally or reluctantly, but as the deliberate outcome of a long pondered and well thought-out program of fundamental changes that he brought to office and immediately began to implement. My argument is that the key to under-standing Curtin and his place in Australian history is that he was a politician gifted with insight into the significance of events, that he came to power just as Australia's structure and its relationship with the rest of the world were ready to change, and that he grasped the authority to move the country in the direction he wanted to go. He understood that the circumstances of war offered him a chance to change the way Australia worked. Though remembered now for bringing the troops home, his primary intellectual interest was economic policy rather than defence policy and the biggest influence on his thinking was not Australia's experience of war against Japan in the 1940s but its experience of the Great Depression in the 1930s. His enduring achievement was not saving Australia from Japan but in creating modern, postwar Australia.

The more we discover about Curtin the more we learn that he was both more and less than the accidental hero of our mythology. As records are opened, as research is extended, the more we see him as the best prepared and trained political leader of his generation: an intelligent, sensible, talented and practical professional politician with a clear and instinctive grasp of the ways of power and the rare gift of understanding the course of great events and his own place in them. We can acknowledge MacArthur's role in commanding Allied forces without diminishing Curtin's role as war leader, and we can also acknowledge Chifley's role as Treasurer while crediting Curtin with a far greater role in the economic management of the war and in the creation of postwar Australia. There is very much more to the Curtin story than saying no to Churchill and Roosevelt—and somewhat less to that refusal than we commonly suppose.

2

Saint Jack

The obscuring legend of Curtin at war begins with his diffidence. In his history of the Commonwealth Parliament Gavin Souter calls Curtin 'the reluctant Prime Minister', and it is certainly true that for a professional politician he was unusually patient in his pursuit of office. As Opposition Leader in the 1940 federal election he famously refused to stand for another if he had lost his seat of Fremantle, and for a while it looked as if he *had* lost. Journalist and member of the House of Representatives for Eden Monaro Alan Fraser claimed that as Opposition Leader Curtin told him Robert Menzies would make a better wartime PM than he would himself. Curtin's longtime private secretary Fred McLaughlin thought of him as a man of principle 'who never sought office'. His reluctance to accept power was, in McLaughlin's view, an aspect of his saintliness. This idea of the reluctant leader is part of the legend in which

Curtin's reputation has been imprisoned. A diffident Opposition Leader thrust into power by the Government's collapse is made great by the war with Japan—and is now remembered for little else.

The facts of Curtin's life don't invite the conclusion that he was a reluctant politician. He scrambled into prominence on his intelligence and socialist conviction as a young man in Melbourne, spent all his life in the Labor movement (including marrying into another Labor family) and from the age of 26 in its employ, repeatedly attempted to enter Federal Parliament despite repeated rejections. He took to serious drinking when he was refused a place in the first ministry of the first Labor Government he had any opportunity to join. From the backbench of the Federal Parliamentary Labor Party he became a major force in the debate on the Depression, offered himself as Leader of the Party as soon as the position became vacant, fought Prime Minister Menzies vehemently as Leader of the Opposition through the 1940 election, refused office in a coalition Government that would have included Menzies and, far from responding to the collapse of the Fadden Government and his own coming appointment as Prime Minister with awe and humility, welcomed it with a glad telegram to his wife. It would be, he cheerfully wrote, her 'birthday gift'.

He did indeed publicly refuse to seek the seat of a colleague if he lost Fremantle in 1940. His daughter remembered that he said, 'I shall not chase my destiny. If Fremantle, which sent me to the Federal Parliament, rejects me from the Federal Parliament, that will be the end of

politics for me'. In the event his refusal was not tested—
he held the seat—but the episode appeared to confirm
Curtin's indifference to power. His daughter also remembered, however, that he refused a proposal that would have
taken him out of politics. Thinking Curtin had lost the
seat, Prime Minister Menzies offered to appoint him High
Commissioner to New Zealand. It was a generous offer,
Curtin said, but one he promptly turned down. According
to his daughter, named Elsie after her mother, 'he had
already determined, if he lost the Fremantle seat, that he
could not depart the Australian political scene even if it
meant filling a lesser role'.

Feigning lack of personal ambition was part of the
etiquette of political struggle, more widely observed in
Curtin's day than our own. There is compelling evidence
that Curtin's apparent reluctance disguised the strength of
his ambition and his determination to win power on his
own terms, and that he was less of a saint and more of a
professional politician than the legend allows.

It suited the newspaper allies of Prime Minister Robert
Menzies to take Curtin's modesty at face value. With
Australia at war, Hitler triumphant in Europe and his own
position relying on the uncertain votes of independents in
Parliament, Menzies proposed a national coalition
Government for Australia on the model of the national
Government of Labor and the Conservatives in the United
Kingdom. Curtin refused. Menzies and the newspapers
continued to exert pressure on Curtin, and the national
Government proposal also found friends in the Labor

caucus. Eager for office, Labor frontbencher Bert Evatt pressed for a coalition with the conservatives, hinting that Curtin's refusal showed he was reluctant to accept the responsibility of power. In a 24 May 1941 letter to the wealthy and disreputable Melbourne Labor power broker John Wren, Evatt complained bitterly that 'Curtin's complete lack of willpower' was keeping Labor's frontbenchers from the ministry. But Curtin understood Menzies' political circumstances better than Evatt did. He knew Menzies was unpopular with his own party and that only a national Government could both keep him in office and also allow him to return to London to join the British War Cabinet. Curtin refused on the very sensible ground that Labor would bear responsibility for what it could not control, and that it would not be able to enact any of the social reforms its supporters expected. Remembering the agony of Labor's Scullin Government as it struggled during the Depression, blocked by a hostile upper house from implementing the policies in which it believed, then broken by conflicts within the party and losing office in a landslide, he declined to let history repeat itself. His refusal of a coalition with Menzies, of fetters on Labor's authority to undertake a massive transformation of Australian society, is central to understanding Curtin. He did not refuse power through timidity. He refused it through ambition.

Far from being alone in declining Menzies' request, Curtin was almost unanimously supported in the Labor movement. It was long-held Labor policy to refuse coalitions, a policy Curtin himself had affirmed and reaffirmed from his earliest days in the party. At a Political Labor Council (predecessor to the Victorian Labor Party) meeting as early as 1908 he had successfully moved that the party not enter into alliance with other parties. In writing about the Labor Party split on conscription in 1917 he had reiterated that, 'All through its existence as a separate political party Labor has had to insist on no alliance being made', both as a way of making the platform clear to voters and as a discipline on leaders who might otherwise opportunistically accept office. Within the Labor Party the view had not changed in 1940 and 1941. Later Minister for Labour in the Whitlam Government, Clyde Cameron was there as a young delegate from South Australia when Curtin spoke to an Australian Workers Union convention in Sydney in 1941. Federal Secretary Clarrie Fallon staged a rousing demonstration of support for the Opposition Leader. When Evatt spoke the following day the disciplined ranks of the AWU officials sat silently through his speech and cheered wildly only when Fallon, with Evatt sitting uncomfortably nearby, announced the implacable opposition of the largest union in the Labor Party to any coalition with the Nationals.

Like Evatt, Menzies spread the story of Curtin's reluctance to take power. Writing just after World War II began to Stanley Bruce, a former Australian Prime Minister who was then Australian High Commissioner in London, Menzies claimed that 'Curtin has privately made it clear to me . . . that his own greatest ambition is to remain Leader of the Opposition for the duration of war'. This is a very serious claim, implying as it does that Curtin was cowardly and irresponsible. He was after all Leader of the Opposition, of the alternative Government, and every sitting day made a claim on the Prime Minister's position that Menzies says he had no intention of redeeming. We do know that Curtin was modest enough to entertain doubts about his ability to govern, but he had fought one very effective campaign as Opposition Leader and would the following year fight another that brought Labor to within a few seats of office. It is anyway hard to believe he would confide to his chief political opponent what amounted to a cowardly refusal to accept leadership in time of war. Curtin preferred to be leader of a united Opposition than a divided Government, and events would prove he made the right decision.

Menzies' remark suggests instead a wilful misunderstanding of Curtin's abilities and intentions that Curtin in some secret, duplicitous place in his heart may have encouraged him to cultivate. Menzies and Curtin treated each other with formal courtesy and the appearance of good fellowship, but they were opponents in a rough game. In private conversation with American officials during the war Menzies described the Curtin Government as 'scum' while publicly maintaining a cordial relationship with Curtin. To reporters Curtin privately made fun of Menzies' claim to infallibility in constitutional matters, pointing out Menzies' meagre results on these cases in appearances before the Privy Council.

Contemporary political commentary in Sydney and Melbourne newspapers often portrayed Opposition Leader Curtin as timid and uncertain. Once in office, however, Curtin displayed much more energy and purpose than Menzies. The newspapers that had scorned him as timid transformed him from reluctant Opposition Leader to trustworthy Prime Minister who understood and shared the fears and anxiety of his people. A year after he became Prime Minister, the *Sydney Morning Herald* described him as a 'miraculously changed person'. It may be, as one writer argues, that as Prime Minister 'John Curtin's public profile was the product of a propaganda campaign during a period of media censorship', but it is also true that in its pursuit of a national coalition Government the press chose to mistake his character as Opposition Leader.

Curtin and his press secretary Don Rodgers may well have contributed to the transformation of the Prime Minister's image once in office. Even the story of Curtin's sleepless vigil has the hint of spin. It grows in the telling, like a fable. Frank Green had his story, but it was widely known elsewhere. Clyde Cameron recalls being told a version of the story by Curtin's Air Minister, Arthur Drakeford. Journalist Alan Reid also wrote an account of what was evidently a widely repeated story at the time. So many and various are these stories that one suspects Don Rodgers played up the story of Curtin's vigil. So successful was the story that it has obscured Curtin's greater achievements and real interests.

A complicated man, Curtin was not as he seemed and not as we remember him. Even people close to Curtin saw him in strikingly different ways. Perhaps because they themselves had different temperaments; perhaps because Curtin had different aspects to his nature, his two closest and most senior staff members seemed to know a different boss. His private secretary, Fred McLaughlin, was a member of the militantly Christian Moral Rearmament Association. He not only later insisted that Curtin had never sought office, but that he was also a Christian who returned to God on his deathbed. His press secretary, Don Rodgers, had known Curtin longer. Like Curtin, Rodgers was himself moody, suffering from long spells of despondency alternating with spells of exhilaration. He recalled Curtin as 'not only a great wartime leader but also a very astute politician' who 'knew his politics and how to play them'. In contrast with McLaughlin, Rodgers was more interested in Curtin the sinner than Curtin the saint. He argued that Curtin was not, as was widely supposed, an alcoholic. Rather, he said, Curtin was a 'cheap drunk' and in the melancholy circumstances of the Scullin Government, which held office for two years during the Depression, 'a crying drunk'. In another of those fine distinctions Rodgers evidently enjoyed, he said that Curtin was 'never an atheist or an agnostic— he was a rationalist'.

Some of Curtin's characteristics do not quite fit the saintly but pallid character described by his private secretary. In a vehement mood his rough tongue was sometimes shocking, even to a politician with as little delicacy of mind as NSW Premier Jack Lang. Curtin had 'a bullock driver's command of banned adjectives', Lang felt compelled to record in his account of the Depression. His daughter recalled him using some very bad language while talking on the phone at their home in Cottesloe. He also had a touch of sardonic humour. Curtin was notoriously frightened of flying, and travelled whenever he could by car or train or boat. (He never learned to drive a car.) In 1944 he was obliged to travel by flying boat to a London conference. On the 20-hour flight from Bermuda to Ireland he told McLaughlin that only three things would get them through—the skill of the pilots, the rotation of the Earth and God Almighty. McLaughlin doesn't seem to have had a lively sense of humour because he later cited this remark as evidence of Curtin's Christian beliefs. Curtin's jokes were dry. Speaking in the Guildhall, London, in 1944, he told a story about a man who was reluctant to migrate to Australia because, he said, that is where convicts went. As the audience chuckled uncertainly he added that the man went anyway, and when he married an Australian she refused to visit England because, she said, that is where convicts came from.

Curtin could handle a political scalpel. As Prime Minister he was sorely tried by two of his ministers, Eddie Ward and Arthur Calwell. He told reporters after his 1943 election win—the biggest two-chamber victory since Federation—that he had given Arthur Calwell the information portfolio because he was always fighting the newspapers and now must learn to live with them, and had given the troublesome

Eddie Ward Transport and Territories because, as he said, 'the Army has the transport and the Japs have the territories'. Later in the war he gleefully told reporters he had sent both the colourful and egocentric External Affairs Minister Bert Evatt and the more pedestrian Deputy Prime Minister Frank Forde to the San Francisco United Nations conference, waiting until Evatt was well on his way before cabling that Forde was to be in charge.

Reading today the accounts of the Curtin background press briefings that Melbourne *Herald* Canberra Press Gallery reporter Harold Cox sent to his boss, Keith Murdoch, we are also struck by Curtin's candour. He gave the latest troops numbers in France, for example, and agreed that progress was less than expected. He openly mentioned what he said was a 'secret strategic' route from Perth to Colombo—which was then the air route to the UK—designed to avoid the Japanese in the Netherlands East Indies. And with the Manhattan project then shrouded in the utmost secrecy Curtin told Cox, who told Keith Murdoch, who could make of it what he would, that 'by an agreement reached in London, the Commonwealth Government would develop deposits of uranium bearing ore in South Australia and supply the whole output to the UK for war purposes'. There was a world shortage of the metal, Curtin told the reporters, 'and the metal is now vitally necessary for scientific purposes associated with the war'.

As an icon for later generations of Labor supporters, Curtin had many imperfections. He developed what proved to be prescient ideas about defence, and particularly the importance of air power. He had long focused on the threat from Japan. He was not, however, a prophet. Through the 1930s he persistently misunderstood Russia, he opposed sanctions against Italy when it invaded Ethiopia and, like many others, slid imperceptibly from disapproval of the World War I Versailles peace settlement to approval of the appeasement policies of British Prime Ministers Stanley Baldwin and Neville Chamberlain. He certainly did not think German Nazism or Italian fascism threats that required an Australian response. As late as the 1938 Munich crisis, Curtin argued that Australia should not be involved in any European war and, even after Germany invaded Poland and war was declared, opposed the sending of Australian forces overseas.

Though an internationalist and for much of his life a socialist, he was also a unquestioning exponent of the attitudes of his times. He did not copy the views of his close friend and political ally Frank Anstey, a Victorian Member of the House of Representatives, who believed the world's problems were caused by Jews in high finance. But he was a lifelong supporter of the White Australia Policy. One of Curtin's arguments against conscription for overseas service during World War I was that it would so deplete the white population of Australia it would be necessary to bring in Asians and blacks. In the war against Japan he portrayed Australia as the outpost of white civilisation in the Pacific, resisting the Asiatic races. In a national broadcast on Australia Day 1942 he concluded a speech about the menace of Japan with the thought that, 'This Australia is for Australians; it is a White Australia, with God's blessing we will keep it so'. Curtin was of course not unusual in these views. Indeed, it would have been impossible in the mainstream of Australian politics to espouse others: White Australia was as much an economic doctrine as a racial doctrine. During the secret sessions of Parliament in February 1942, Curtin explained that the American Army forces coming to Australia would bring with them a problem that, on the whole, he thought it best to overlook. 'It may be added for your information', he told a secret session on 19 February, 'that American Army formations contain certain units of coloured troops who are, of course, called up for military service as American citizens. The Government felt it would be quite incorrect for it to lay down any stipulation regarding the admission of coloured troops to this country when such a course would emasculate the organisation of the American forces being sent to this region'. Curtin's concern was shared by the Opposition. Responding to a cable from Australian Washington representative Richard Casey, the Advisory War Council decided on 12 January 1942 that 'the Commonwealth should not agree to the proposal that a proportion of United States troops despatched should be coloured'. The United States apparently objected because on 20 January the Advisory War Council acknowledged that the US government could determine the composition of the forces but Casey was instructed to say the Council assumed the United States 'would have regard to Australian susceptibilities'. A little later it was considered a remarkable concession to agree to the US request to bring in labourers from the Netherlands East Indies to accelerate the building of defences in northern Australia—a project that lapsed when the Japanese took control of the archipelago.

Curtin was not as reluctant a leader, not as saintly in his conduct, not as unprejudiced in his views as the legend tells us. The most enduring of the fables told of Curtin is that he saved Australia from Japanese invasion by insisting on the return of Australian infantry divisions in the Middle East. If he is remembered for nothing else he is remembered for that, yet this most celebrated of his decisions as Prime Minister was also not quite as it seems—and its mythology obscures the much greater place Curtin commands in Australian history.

3

Bringing the
Troops Home

To weigh the significance of the decision to bring the troops home we need to take ourselves back to the ideas of the time, and the events that preceded Curtin's refusal of the joint request of Churchill and Roosevelt. The starting point for this reconsideration is very simple. For Curtin the Japanese attack in the Pacific was the most threatening event in the history of Australia; for Churchill it was the best news he had yet heard in the war.

When Curtin became Prime Minister in early October 1941 three Australian army divisions were fighting Germans and Italians in the Middle East, and another stood on guard against a Japanese attack in Malaya. As Opposition Leader Curtin had initially opposed sending Australian troops to the Middle East and he was deeply concerned by the threat of war with Japan. But while there were a few premonitory disputes it was the Japanese attack on Pearl Harbor on 7 December 1941 that opened up a new area of discord between Curtin and Churchill. The entry of Japan into the war created a serious conflict between the central national interests of Australia and the central national interests of Britain, hitherto closely aligned.

In December 1941 the war in Europe hung in the balance. Germany controlled most of Western Europe and, in Churchill's opinion, would soon defeat the Soviet Union. In North Africa Rommel had been driven back but was regrouping for a new campaign in which he would regain lost ground. In the Atlantic German submarines would soon be sinking British and American cargo ships faster than they could be built and crewed. But the moment Churchill heard the news of the Japanese attack on Pearl Harbor he knew that however gloomy things looked, Britain could not be lost and sooner or later Germany would be beaten. 'So we had won after all!' was his immediate and heartfelt response to the first radio news bulletin. The Japanese attack had brought the might of the United States into the war against Germany. 'Hitler's fate was sealed,' Churchill later wrote of the news. 'Mussolini's fate was sealed. As for the Japanese, they would be ground to powder.' While Churchill was celebrating, Curtin was meeting with an appalled War Cabinet in Melbourne to discuss the looming threat to Australia's survival.

For his part Hitler was also delighted by the news of Pearl Harbor. He thought (probably correctly) that it was anyway only a matter of time before the United States came into the war against Germany, and Japan would now tie the US fleet down in the Pacific. Hitler's plan was therefore to beat the Soviet Union before the United States brought its power to bear in Europe. He would then be master of Europe, with a reasonable chance that the Allies would sooner or later have to make peace with him. It followed that Churchill's aim after Pearl Harbor was to make sure the United States was *not* tied down in the Pacific. Japan was in the North Pacific, it was much less powerful than Germany, it could not attack the North American mainland and it would exhaust itself if it attacked Russia. Japan might for a time hold all its Pacific conquests without delaying the Allied victory over Germany by a day. The main threat Japan's entry to the war presented to Britain was that it might force the United States to divert to the Pacific resources that could otherwise be used in the war against Germany. Churchill was determined to prevent that diversion, a policy that brought him into conflict with Curtin.

Japan did, however, present one small but significant direct risk to Britain. Controlling Greece, allied with Italy and with Spain wavering, there was a real risk Germany could take control of the Mediterranean and capture the oil supplies of the Middle East by sweeping south from a defeated Russia. If Japan could invade India through Burma and if its navy could dominate the Indian Ocean as it now dominated the Pacific, German and Japanese forces could link up in Iran and its navies would control the Mediterranean and the Indian Ocean.

But while a Japanese attack through Burma into India could help Germany, a Japanese invasion of Australia could not. Australia was very big but mostly desert. It had plenty of meat, grain, wool and coal, but little oil and few other known natural resources. Conquering Australia led nowhere, except perhaps to the conquest of New Zealand. It would extend Japan's defence perimeter and dramatically increase the vulnerability of its forces with no impact on the war against Germany. Churchill was accordingly less worried about an invasion of Australia than an invasion of Ceylon, Burma and perhaps India. It was in fulfilment of this strategic concept that within a week of Japan's attack on Pearl Harbor Churchill himself, then steaming across the Atlantic on the battleship *Duke of York* to confer with Roosevelt, told the British Chiefs of Staff to look at sending the Australian 6th Division from the Middle East to help meet the Japanese threat to the British Far East base at Singapore.

Churchill's determination to keep the US focused on Germany rather than Japan was embodied in the 'Germany First' agreement between himself and Roosevelt even before Japan came into the war. The understanding was immediately threatened, however, by the indignation of the American public over Pearl Harbor. It was also threatened by Curtin's insistence that Australia should participate directly in Allied decisions on the Pacific war, which would necessarily be made primarily in Washington. Threatened with imminent attack by Japan, Australia would certainly not accept a view that the war against Germany came first. Churchill resented and resisted Curtin's famous 27 December 1941 Melbourne *Herald* appeal to the United States, but not because of Curtin's call for US support. It was already the policy of Australia and the United Kingdom that the United States would have the primary role in the Pacific in the event of war with Japan. It was part of Churchill's understanding with Roosevelt that the United States would assume responsibility for Australia. The dispute between Curtin and Churchill was not about the role of the United States in the war, but about whether Australia had a direct voice in US planning. Churchill did not care for Curtin's declaration in the *Herald* that Australia looked to the United States free of any pangs as to its traditional kinship with the United Kingdom, but his deeper objection was to Curtin's statement in the same piece that 'the Australian government regards the Pacific struggle as primarily one in which the United States and Australia must have the fullest say in the direction of the democracies' fighting plan'. Curtin also wrote that 'we refuse to accept the dictum that the Pacific struggle must be treated as a subordinate segment of the general conflict' and, most woundingly, 'we know that Australia can go and Britain can still hold on'—a judgement Churchill knew to be correct.

To Churchill these words were a direct challenge. He wanted to run the relationship between the UK and her dominions, and the United States. He wanted to keep the

United States focused on the war in Europe rather than on the war in the Pacific. He wanted Australia's views put to the Americans through him. Curtin wanted to put them directly. On 9 January 1942 Churchill proposed that the orders of British General Archibald Wavell, the supreme commander of the Allied forces in the Southwest Pacific, be received from Washington. Those orders would embody agreements between Churchill and the President—with Churchill responsible for ascertaining the views of Australia, New Zealand and the Dutch government-in-exile. Churchill proposed to create in London a purely advisory Pacific War Council on which Australia would be represented, but which would not include the United States. With the support of the Australian Advisory War Council and the War Cabinet Curtin strongly objected to the proposed arrangement, instead seeking 'an appropriate joint body' based in Washington and including the United States. He insisted that Churchill convey his views on the higher direction of the war to Roosevelt.

While Curtin and Churchill argued over the higher direction of the Pacific war, the Japanese forced British, Australian and Indian troops down the Malayan peninsula toward Singapore. The island base was to become the next flashpoint in the deepening dispute between Churchill and Curtin.

Since European settlement Australian defence planning had depended on Empire Defence, in which the dominions would contribute troops and money to the defence of the UK and its dominions, while relying on the British fleet for their own defence. As wartime secretary of the Australian Department of Defence and of the War Cabinet Sir Frederick Shedden wrote, 'the conception of Empire Defence in which Australians had been brought to believe was an impregnable Singapore base with a fleet of capital ships based thereon'.

Before Japan came into the war Churchill's priorities, he later wrote, were the 'defence of the Island', the Middle East, supplies to Russia 'and, last of all, resistance to a Japanese assault'. His rationale was quite straightforward. If Japan did come into the war, the United States would probably be in. But if the United States were not in, there was no means anyway of defending the 'Empire in the East'. He added almost as an afterthought that if Japan invaded Australia or New Zealand, 'the Middle East should be sacrificed to the defence of our kith and kin', a contingency 'we all regarded as remote and improbable'. Even while Japan's battle fleet was preparing for Pearl Harbor, the British Government doubted Japan would come into the war, at least in 1941. Attending an Australian Advisory War Council meeting on 16 October 1941, for example, British Commander in Chief of the Far East Sir Robert Brooke-Popham said Japan would be unable to commence a large-scale attack in the south for three months. If and when it did attack, Japan lacked aerodromes in the south, so British forces in Malaya would have air superiority. Churchill cabled Curtin on 25 October that he was 'still inclined to think Japan would not run into war with the American-British-Chinese-Dutch powers unless or until Russia was decisively broken'. But if Japan did come into the war, the British Government assured Australia, Singapore would be held. During an Australian Advisory War Council meeting on 7 November British Minister in the Far East Duff Cooper said, 'it had always been the intention of the United Kingdom government to reinforce the Far East, and they were prepared to abandon the Mediterranean altogether if this were necessary to hold Singapore'.

The British were certainly not prepared to abandon the Mediterranean, but Churchill did not leave Singapore defenceless. On the contrary he responded to Australia's concerns about the Japanese threat by sending to Singapore the modern battlecruisers *Prince of Wales* and *Repulse* before Japan's entry to the war. With other, older ships already based in Singapore they made up the squadron of six big warships mentioned in prewar planning for the Singapore base. This 'appeared satisfactory' to Curtin, according to Shedden, and the Australian Prime Minister cabled Churchill on 31 October that the ships 'should force Japan into the position of again weighing most seriously the consequences of further aggression either northwards or southwards'. The *Prince of Wales* was the newest and most powerful cruiser in the British fleet. Churchill himself had only recently sailed across the Atlantic on it for his Newfoundland meeting with Roosevelt in August 1941. Acknowledging Curtin's message, Churchill cabled on 2 November that he was 'very glad that Curtin was pleased about the big ship. There was nothing like having something that could catch and kill anything'. The ships would arrive in Singapore on 2 December 1941.

Not only was Singapore provided with the promised fleet before Japan entered the war; Malaya was also well defended, by forces including Australia's 8th Division. Throughout Japan's rapid conquest of Malaya and Singapore its troops were easily outnumbered by the Allied defenders. Neither the ships nor the troops, however, proved remotely adequate to meet the Japanese challenge. The *Prince of Wales* and the *Repulse* were sunk by Japanese warplanes off the Malaya coast on 10 December. With overwhelming air superiority, untroubled by the supposed lack of airfields, Japanese troops rapidly advanced down the Malay peninsula using bicycles, small tanks and aircraft in ways the British command did not expect, and with skill they did not expect.

The British misjudged the likelihood of Japan entering the war, and then its ability to fight. The looming defeat in Singapore then shattered Australia's confidence in British security guarantees, and triggered another and more difficult dispute between Curtin and Churchill. The British Prime Minister realised Singapore had ceased to be of strategic importance as soon as the *Prince of Wales* and the *Repulse* were lost. Its capacity to deter Japan depended entirely on the fleet based there. Singapore was not intended to be impregnable to land attack, nor could it be since its water supplies depended on Malaya. There could not be a land attack so long as the British fleet controlled the seas. Without that control, however, Singapore was not only useless but also indefensible. The northern side of the island was open to attack and, as Churchill discovered to his dismay, it remained undefended even as the Japanese moved into southern Malaya.

A few weeks after the loss of the two big ships Stanley Bruce, the Australian representative in London, alerted the Australian Government to Churchill's view that Singapore ought to be abandoned and the troops evacuated. Curtin was aware of this at home in Perth in the second half of January. In the Prime Minister's name and no doubt with his approval External Affairs minister Evatt cabled Churchill on 23 January that Australia would regard the abandonment of Singapore as an 'inexcusable betrayal'. Curtin was no doubt thinking of his disputes with Churchill about access to Washington and the defence of Singapore when he said in an Australia Day broadcast three days later that 'No single nation can afford to risk its future on the infallibility of one man, and no nation can afford to submerge its right of speaking for itself because of the assumed omniscience of another'.

Curtin and his ministers were outraged by the possibility the UK would abandon the defence of Singapore, but by late January its strategic value was wholly imaginary. It was a naval base without a navy—and without a navy the armies retreating to Singapore could neither be reinforced nor evacuated. Reservations about the invincibility of the British fleet lay behind the Australian Army's long held objections to an Empire Defence strategy based on Singapore. The Americans correctly saw that it was not essential and did not agree that its fall would be crucial for a war against Japan in the Pacific. Its fall was far more significant for the loss of prestige than for the loss of strategic advantage. For Australia as well, the loss was more symbolic than actual. It symbolised the dissolution of the military alliance between the United Kingdom and Australia in the Pacific and dramatised the fact that their national interests were no longer aligned. Its fall also meant that Churchill's prestige with the Australians was deflated at a time of conflicts over other issues, including the destination of the 7th Division.

But Australians could not blame Churchill for the loss of Singapore. Far from betraying commitments to Australia, Churchill committed more land and sea forces to the defence of Malaya and Singapore than he thought wise or that could be justified by strategic imperatives—and he did so largely at Australia's insistence. Churchill was quite right in wanting to abandon Singapore in mid-January. Coming not long after the sharp dispute over Australia's access to the Pacific war command structure in Washington, however, the fall of Singapore clouded the relationship between Curtin and Churchill at a critical time. They were just about to begin five days of argument over whether troops of Australia's 7th Division, now sailing across the Indian Ocean, should be landed in Burma or Australia. Part of Churchill's insistence in coming days that Australian troops be sent to Burma rather than to Australia was out of a sense that Curtin was at least partly responsible for the disaster of the capture of the British and Australian armies in Singapore. Part of the strength of Curtin's refusal was because after the fall of Singapore he had rightly lost confidence in British security assurances.

Curtin and Churchill had disagreed over access to Washington and now over Singapore. Meanwhile, the ultimate destination of Australian troops sailing back from the Middle East was slowly working its way up as the dramatic dispute that would become a legend of Australian nationhood.

Within days of Japan's entry to the war questions had been raised about the deployment of the three Australian battle-trained divisions then fighting in the Middle East. As early as 17 December, for example, Major General Gordon Bennett, the Australian commander in Malaya, asked to be reinforced with one Australian division from the Middle East. Curtin informed Churchill of this on 20 December. But he had had no need to press Churchill on the return of troops from the Middle East, because Churchill had asked the British Chiefs of Staff as early as 15 December to consider sending an Australian division from Palestine to Singapore.

On Christmas Day 1941—two days before Curtin's appeal to the United States was published in the Melbourne *Herald*—while a guest at the White House, Churchill cabled Curtin requesting that one Australian division be moved to Singapore. During a meeting of the Advisory War Council on 31 December Curtin mentioned a cable from Churchill dated 27 December proposing the transfer of an AIF division from the Middle East, either to India to replace troops that had already been sent to Malaya, or directly to Singapore. Curtin said he was not in favour of sending the troops to India, and the Advisory War Council agreed. The Council resolved that if a specific request for the transfer of an AIF division from the Middle East to the Far East (which meant Malaya, Singapore and the then Netherlands East Indies) were received, the Government should approve it.

On 3 January the British Government formally asked the Australian Government to allow two Australian divisions to be sent from the Middle East to join the American, British, Dutch, Australian (ABDA) command that was being hastily organised in Java under Wavell, whom Churchill had earlier that year sacked from the Middle East command and sent to India. On 5 January 1942 the Advisory War Council and then the Australian War Cabinet approved the transfer of the 6th and 7th to the Netherlands East Indies. To this point there was no dispute between Curtin and Churchill over the return of troops, on which they were agreed.

While Curtin and his colleagues anxiously followed reports of the Japanese advance down the Malayan peninsula and through the Philippines, the first of the Australian troops from the Middle East put to sea. Code-named Stepsister, the operation transported 64 000 troops and their equipment in 70 ships from the Middle East to the Far East between January and April. To speed the movement the heavy equipment was often sent separately from the troops, an important consideration in the later dispute over their deployment. The first eight ships reached Colombo at the end of January and left for the Netherlands East Indies on 3 February.

One of the biggest transports, the *Mount Vernon*, a 34 600 ton US tourist liner converted to war use, left Port Tewfik, Egypt, on 8 February. Brigadier L. Prowse of the 25th Brigade recalled that the cabins were satisfactory, as were the meals. They were more satisfactory for the Brigadier than for the privates. One private recalled that the officers travelled in cabins attended by servants, the non-commissioned officers travelled in the equivalent of second class, while the rest travelled in converted cargo holds. The beds were fold-up iron frames and 'a man's territory was his bed'.

While the *Mount Vernon* and the other ships of Step-sister sailed east, Australian leaders pondered the vessels' destination. War Cabinet had agreed that the two divisions would be sent to defend the Netherlands East Indies. As the weeks went by, Australian officers sent ahead to join Wavell in the Netherlands East Indies began to realise that without control of the skies and the seas, Java and Sumatra could not be held. Appointed under Wavell as general officer commanding the first Australian corps, Australian Lieutenant General John Lavarack wrote to the Chief of the Australian General Staff Vernon Sturdee on 6 February suggesting the decision to land the Australian troops in Sumatra be reviewed. Two days later Major General Charles Lloyd, administrative officer to Wavell, wrote in stronger terms to Sturdee condemning the proposal. Once Japanese troops landed on Singapore on 8 February, Wavell and the Australian command could rapidly conclude that the Netherlands East Indies could not be held and that Australian troops sent there would be lost.

Of the Australian defence chiefs only Sturdee was Australian, and the Army had a long history of scepticism of the value of the British naval shield and of the Singapore naval base. To the Army, the Australian troops would likely be lost if they tried to stop the Japanese in Southeast Asia and, once lost, Australia was defenceless. How much better, considering that risk, to bring the troops to Australia where if necessary they could fight on their home ground with all the advantages of transport, supplies, manoeuvrability and a friendly population?

The Australian Army leadership's growing doubts about a landing in Java were put directly to Curtin. Sturdee called Curtin as soon as he received the letter Lloyd had sent on 8 February. On 13 February, with the fall of Singapore evidently imminent and well aware of the Army's resistance to sending the 6th and 7th to Java, Curtin called for a new strategic appreciation from both the British and Australian general staffs. Two days later, as Allied forces in Singapore surrendered and the survivors of the Australian 8th Division began their march toward Changi prison camp, Sturdee read Curtin over a secure phone a cable from Lavarack, then later that day cabled his view that if deployed in the Netherlands East Indies the troops would probably be lost, and even if not lost Java was not the place to make a stand.

Curtin was not slow to respond. He had evidently been working on Saturday 14 February on a cable to Churchill, which was sent the next day. Even at this point he did not insist but rather put forward for consideration that the Australian troops at sea should now be diverted to Australia rather than continue to the Netherlands East Indies. The following day the Australian Chiefs of Staff recommended that the troops come home—a decision effectively made by Sturdee, with the concurrence of his English colleagues. By the middle of the month, therefore, the Army and Curtin were working in close alliance.

By this point Churchill had also dropped his request that Australian troops returning from the Middle East be sent to Singapore or Java. With the rapid Japanese victories, neither destination any longer made sense. As the prospect of holding Singapore faded, however, Churchill's thoughts had moved in a quite different direction. He thought there was little danger of the Japanese invading Australia and that the United States could, anyway, defend it. Some or all of the returning Australian troops, he thought, should block the Japanese invasion of Burma. Already on ships in the region, already battle trained, they could prevent the Japanese reaching India. On 17 February he told the British Chiefs that an Australian division should be diverted to Burma, after Wavell had advised on 16 February that Java could not be held and recommended Australian troops should be diverted to Burma. On the same day, Churchill cabled Roosevelt that Burma was the most important theatre after the loss of Singapore, hinting that

Australian troops could be diverted to strengthen its defences. On 18 February Page and Bruce reported British War Cabinet and Pacific War Council discussions in London that had urged Australia to allow the 7th Division to be committed to Burma, a proposal Bruce and Page both supported. The British view was soon backed up (at Churchill's instigation) with a cable from Roosevelt, which initiated the five-day cable war between the British and Australian prime ministers.

Armed with the chiefs' recommendation, Curtin had cabled Churchill on Tuesday 17 February with an unequivocal request that arrangements be made to transport the AIF now in Bombay and the ships following to Australia. Copies were also sent to Wavell and to Earle Page, the Australian Government representative (when Australian matters were being discussed) to the British cabinet. That same day Curtin convened the Full Cabinet for a meeting in Sydney at 10.30 a.m. He told the ministers Australia needed to rely on its own resources and that it was now 'impractical' to give 'substantial aid to countries outside Australia'. Full Cabinet then authorised War Cabinet to take steps for a full mobilisation of Australian resources for the war. Curtin later spoke at a war loan rally in Martin Place. Within three-quarters of an hour of finishing his speech he was admitted to St Vincent's hospital, suffering, so it was reported, from gastritis resulting from prolonged nervous strain. That same day the War Cabinet ordered the 'complete mobilisation of all resources, human and material, to ensure the defence of Australia'.

Up to the final five days there was little dispute between Curtin and Churchill, or between the Government members of the Advisory War Council and the Opposition leaders. But by Wednesday 18 February, with Singapore lost and resistance in the Netherlands East Indies crumbling, Curtin was fighting both Churchill and the Australian Opposition leaders. On the day the Advisory War Council discussed the choice between Australia and Burma, Opposition frontbencher Percy Spender argued for Burma, saying the Burma road between India and China was of 'vital importance' in sustaining Chinese resistance to Japan. He said England had been immobilised by the threat of invasion, and they must resist the same happening in Australia. Curtin was still in hospital but Evatt said the Prime Minister's view was that the troops should be returned to Australia. The meeting concluded with an agreement to reconvene to discuss the issue at 10 the following morning. The Pacific War Council, however, had meanwhile been meeting in London. The committee included Page, who was persuaded to recommend the Australian divisions go to Burma. Page cabled Curtin on the evening of 18 February, and Curtin immediately replied that the Government was unlikely to change its mind and the convoys should not be committed to Burma.

When the Advisory War Council reconvened on Thursday morning Deputy Prime Minister Frank Forde submitted Curtin's telegrams to Churchill, requesting urgent arrangements for the diversion to Australia of the AIF at Bombay en route to Java. He also requested the return to Australia of the remaining troops at sea and of the 9th Division, still in the Middle East. The Opposition members seized on the cable from Page. Spender, former Prime Ministers Billy Hughes, Artie Fadden and Robert Menzies and the Country Party's John McEwen all supported the recommendation of the Pacific War Council to divert the 7th Division to Burma. The debate was acrimonious, with voices 'raised in anger', according to Spender. Driving home his argument for the return of the troops, Labor cabinet minister John Dedman dramatically announced the news that Darwin had been bombed that morning.

Meeting later that day, the War Cabinet affirmed Curtin's earlier decision and Evatt drafted answering cables to Page. After attempts by Page and the British Government to persuade him to change his mind Curtin reaffirmed the position, cabling Page after midnight on 20 February a four-line message ordering him to act on previous cables.

Some hours earlier, however, at 9 p.m. London time, Churchill had ordered the convoy transporting the Australian troops to head north to Rangoon. A few minutes later he cabled Curtin arguing that the Australian troops were the only ones able to prevent the capture of Rangoon, and cabled Roosevelt urging him to put pressure on Curtin. Churchill did not mention to Curtin that he had already ordered the transports to Rangoon.

With Curtin and Churchill exchanging vigorous cables, the Australian soldiers at sea scented indecision. Thursday 19 February, the day voices were raised on the Advisory

War Council, found Sergeant Ray Ogg of the 2/6th Field Regiment on another of the Stepsister vessels, the *Mathura*, still heading southeast toward Sumatra. 'The boys are getting a bit jittery', Ogg confided to his diary, with the news of the capture of the 8th Division and heavy air raids on Darwin and Java. The ship, he wrote, was 'very much on the alert now and getting into dangerous waters'. On Friday the troops on board heard that Sumatra was finished. There were then 'arguments all over the ship as to whether we were going to Australia or Batavia'. There were arguments all over the *Mount Vernon*, too. It was now sailing to Sumatra. On the night of 17 February, according to the unit record, the ship turned 180 degrees and the following morning it arrived in Colombo. This was the same day Curtin had sent off his first cable asking that the troops be diverted to Australia. The *Orcades* had gone ahead. The *Mount Vernon* would remain in Colombo until the final destination was agreed. At 10 a.m. on 18 February it dropped anchor at Colombo. It was only then that the troops on board learned of the fall of Singapore, three days earlier. Their ship remained in Colombo six days, while the cable war was fought out between Curtin and Churchill.

The drama in Canberra resumed. Just out of hospital, Curtin addressed a secret session of Parliament on Friday afternoon. The speech prepared for Curtin by Shedden is likely to have been close to the text he used. Curtin recalled the defeat of the Allied forces in Malaya and the loss of 18 000 troops with the fall of Singapore just five days before. Australia had suffered, he said, 'the most serious

losses yet experienced in this war'. Even then, Australia was
unclear about the real situation and 'little hope can be held
out of the successful evacuation of any of these forces as
the intention was to fight on in Singapore to the last'. The
Japanese also held the Dutch territories of Borneo, Celebes
and Ambon, and he did not know what had happened to
the Royal Australian Air Force and Army personnel on
Ambon. South Sumatra had already been overrun, an
attack on Java was now imminent, and 'we have been
advised that the prospects of a successful defence of this
island are not good'. In handwriting the text is amended
to add that 'The fall of the Netherlands East Indies will
[bring?] Darwin into the front line of battle'. The issue
now was how the Japanese would proceed. They could
advance on Port Moresby, they could advance along the
chain of islands to Australia's east to cut off the flow of
supplies from the United States, and they would likely
consider both 'as necessary preliminaries to a major attack
on the Australian mainland'. Australia had reinforced Port
Moresby; the Americans were directing forces that could
support New Caledonia.

> The enemy's successes to the north west and north east
> of Australia have brought the enemy to our very gates,
> and Australia is now face to face with the likelihood of
> enemy attacks in force on our own shores. These attacks
> must be repulsed not only to safeguard ourselves but
> to maintain Australia as an Allied base from which

attacks leading to the final defeat of the enemy can be launched.

In these circumstances, he said, the 'Government has given urgent consideration in the [past] few days to the question of the future employment of the AIF [Australian Imperial Force]'. The decision to bring back two divisions from the Middle East had been requested by Churchill. They were intended for the Netherlands East Indies, but in light of the Japanese advance the Government had requested the British Government to 'arrange for the diversion to Australia of the 6th and 7th Divisions and the return to Australia of the 9th Division as soon as possible'. There was no mention in his prepared remarks of Burma as an alternative.

At midnight that night Curtin sent a cable to Page ordering him to act on the previous messages. But while Curtin was telling Parliament the divisions would return to Australia, the convoy under Churchill's orders was steaming to Rangoon. On the *Mathura* Sergeant Ogg recorded that by Sunday 22 February the ship was travelling north, and they were told the destination was Rangoon—'a hot spot with the Japanese attacking strongly'.

Curtin called a special meeting of War Cabinet on 21 February, with cables in from Churchill and Page and an appeal from Roosevelt. Curtin was at this point still unaware that some ships were actually on course for Burma's capital. He told the meeting that if they went against their better judgement they would expose Australia to danger. Chifley pointed out that the Japanese were only 40 miles from Rangoon.

In the early hours of Sunday Curtin replied to Churchill that 'our wishes in regard to the disposition of the AIF in the Pacific theatre have long been known to you' and had not changed. It was only in a cable sent by Churchill that afternoon that Curtin learned of the diversion of the ships. Churchill explained that 'We could not contemplate that you would refuse our request and that of the President'. The convoy was now too far north to proceed to Australia without refuelling, so Australia had a few days to review the position. This would have been received in Australia early Monday morning. From his office that afternoon Curtin cabled Churchill that 'it is quite impossible to reverse a decision which we made with the utmost care and which we have affirmed and reaffirmed'. The message was sent at 5.45 p.m. on Monday. On the same day, Sergeant Ogg recorded that the *Mathura* was now travelling west, and they heard they were going back to Ceylon. The following day the *Mount Vernon* left Colombo. They were told their destination was Fremantle. It would be the first of the ships bringing troops back from the Middle East to reach Australia.

On the same day the *Mount Vernon* left Colombo for Fremantle, Lieutenant General Lavarack told the Advisory War Council that 'the ships conveying the first and second flights of the AIF from the Middle East had not been tactically loaded, and if the first flight had been diverted to Burma, the troops could not have been landed as an effective fighting force . . .'. It would, he said, have taken 21 days to re-sort their equipment.

There is no doubt Curtin's refusal to allow the diversion of the 7th to Burma was the only sensible decision an Australian leader could have made. The extraordinary political action was not Curtin's insistence that the 7th Division troops come home, but the insistence of Menzies and Spender, two of the architects of Australian postwar foreign policy, that they be sent to Burma. Rangoon fell to the Japanese on 8 March. There is little doubt that without air support, without the trucks, tanks and artillery packed in other ships, the Australians committed to the defence of Burma would have been lost, as the troops on board the *Orcades* were soon lost in the Netherlands East Indies. Yet the Opposition members of the Advisory War Council continued to defend their judgement, accusing the Government of cowardice and panic for years afterward.

It was the right decision, but it was not quite the event of Australian lore. The proposal to bring the troops back from the Middle East was actually initiated by Churchill, and the real dispute by the time the leading elements of the 7th Division reached Colombo was whether those elements should be sent to Burma or to Australia. There is no doubt Curtin made the correct decision and that he faced considerable opposition from Churchill, Roosevelt, the Opposition members of the War Cabinet and Australia's minister in London. But he had the solid support of his own War Cabinet, and support from the military command was so strong that one of the Army commanders was said to have threatened to resign if Burma was agreed. There was also no doubt that as Australian Prime Minister the decision was Curtin's to make, not Churchill's or Roosevelt's. Both the British Prime Minister and the US President recognised this. And as Sir Frederick Shedden, the secretary of the War Cabinet and Curtin's principal civilian adviser on military issues, wrote in an unpublished record, 'With Australia under risk, no self respecting Government conscious of its responsibilities could have ignored the recommendation of its military advisers'. It was also overwhelmingly popular. Like most press secretaries Rodgers had little reverence in his makeup, even for such a glorious event as the return of the 6th and 7th Divisions from the Middle East to Australia. He later said admiringly that Curtin's insistence on their return to Australia 'was a very smart move and I should think had a big effect on the 1943 election'.

4

Curtin as Warlord

For all the controversy, the return of those troops did not prove to be quite as critical to Australia's war effort as legend has it. One reason is that Curtin did not in fact bring back most of the troops, or at least not in the early months of 1942. The *Mount Vernon* arrived safely in early March and the other ships of Stepsister soon followed, but a high proportion of the AIF remained elsewhere. Though insisting those leading elements of the 7th be sent to Australia, Curtin had already agreed to the fastest ship, the *Orcades*, going to Java, where the troops were captured. In March Curtin agreed that the 16th and 17th brigades of the 6th Division could remain in Ceylon to support the British Indian Ocean naval buildup based on that island, and they stayed there until mid-July. In June 1942 Rommel captured Tobruk and advanced on Cairo. With reverses in the Allied position in the Middle East the 9th Division was fighting in Syria by July, and would not come home until the beginning of 1943. In June 1942 only four of the eleven brigades Australia had sent overseas had returned. Under continuing pressure from both Roosevelt and Churchill, Curtin had conceded for the 6th and the 9th Divisions what he had rightly refused for the 7th. Churchill wanted Ceylon defended while he built up a British Indian Ocean carrier force that could prevent a seaborne Japanese attack on India. By July the crisis had passed, and the two Australian brigades could be released. Both Roosevelt and Churchill wanted the 9th to remain in the Middle East, and Roosevelt assured Curtin that the United States could secure Australia against attack. Had Australia been invaded before the middle of 1942, the time of maximum Japanese power, around half of the AIF (excluding the captured 8th) would still have been west of Singapore.

The Australian troops Curtin insisted on bringing back were soon in action in Papua, but most of the AIF was still away from Australia when the danger of invasion was greatest. Was the danger, however, quite as great as Curtin warned? There were certainly good grounds for concern, and Australian military authorities did not rule out an invasion. In an appreciation prepared at the end of February the Australian Chiefs of Staff of the armed forces told Curtin they expected Allied resistance in the Netherlands East Indies would end in a week, and that by the third week of March the enemy would have a task force of three divisions ready for a possible attack on Australia's northwest coast. They believed the Japanese had 500–600 aircraft in the Southwest Pacific as well as overwhelming naval superiority. The chiefs thought the Japanese would try to occupy Port Moresby and so command the Coral Sea, and possibly northeastern Australia, the southern Solomons or New Hebrides or New Caledonia, to close off communications across the Pacific between Australia and the United States. They believed Australia needed 25 divisions to resist invasion. It had instead one brigade of troops in Port Moresby, one brigade and two regiments in Darwin, and one division in Queensland. It was also woefully short of planes and pilots. The chiefs reported that Australia had three fighter squadrons, two dive bomber squadrons, and one heavy bomber squadron under training—a total of 60 planes.

This portrayal of Australia as completely unprepared to meet a possible invasion was underlined in accounts of the experience of General Douglas MacArthur, who arrived in Darwin by sea on 17 March and by 20 March was travelling to Adelaide by train. A staff member joined the train a few miles from Adelaide, one of MacArthur's biographers records, and reported to MacArthur that to meet the Japanese threat Australia had 32 000 troops, mostly non-combatants, and a few hundred aircraft, mostly obsolete. Many of its naval ships had been sunk. 'God have mercy on us', MacArthur is said to have remarked, later saying the news was 'the greatest shock and surprise of the whole war'.

This description of a defenceless Australia was useful at the time for seeking more support from the United States and Britain, but the picture was quite untrue—and Curtin would have known it was untrue. When militia units were included in the total, Australia was quite well defended against the likely threat. These were troops who had volunteered or been conscripted for home defence, and undergoing training. Though poorly regarded by the professional soldiers they were comparable in training with the US national guard, which provided the bulk of the US troops coming to Australia. Militia units accounted for the majority of Australian troops who would fight in Papua and New Guinea and were rapidly being equipped with weapons and other resources that matched those of the Japanese or the US troops. Including the militia there were 382 000 in the Australian armed forces in December 1941, and 554 700 by March 1942. Australia's total population was then seven million, so there was the equivalent of one and a half million Australians in the armed forces in 2005.

Some of these armed forces were in the Middle East and not all were in the Army, but looking at the Army alone and only those at home, Australia had a comfortable edge. Again including the militia, by the end of February 1942 there were 271 000 troops in Australia, about half in training in combat units (this does not include the AIF). By the end of March (including the returned 7th Division and some US troops who had arrived) there were 400 000 Army troops. The numbers continued to rapidly increase. By mid-1942 607 000 of 1 529 000 Australian males between 18 and 45 had enlisted. There were then 98 000 US Army and Air Corps in Australia, and Australia had

48 000 troops still in the Middle East. The buildup of military forces in Australia accelerated through 1942, with new call-ups, extended training, the arrival of the American 41st and 32nd Divisions and the return home of the remainder of the 7th and part of the 6th. The US troops swelled the numbers but, but as one military historian concluded, even 'before the first American divisions arrived the number of men in khaki in Australia exceeded the number of troops the Japanese were to have deployed in the area from the East Indies to the Solomons at any time in 1942'.

The Japanese had a local and temporary superiority in planes and ships, but certainly not in manpower. They would have been able to land and harass but they did not then or later have enough troops to invade Australia. After the war and before his execution, former Prime Minister Tojo insisted that Japan had no plans to invade Australia. He said, 'We never had enough troops to do so . . . we expected to occupy all of New Guinea, to maintain Rabaul as a holding base and to raid northern Australia by air. But actual physical invasion—no, at no time'.

Did Curtin lie about the Japanese threat? An attack on Australia was certainly an option Curtin could not dismiss. The Japanese high command examined two major alternatives of attacking Midway and Hawaii, or attacking the Solomons and Samoa and blockading Australia and raiding its coast. 'At the beginning of the war', writes one historian of the Japanese decision-making, 'the Navy argued for an invasion of Australia. The Army turned it down, claiming that the necessary shipping was unavailable. In truth, the Army wished to keep its forces along the Soviet border in Manchuria so they could profit from the anticipated collapse in Moscow'. We now know that factions in Japan's military command in Tokyo were pushing for an extension of Japan's defence perimeter to Australia. We also know these factions were over-ruled. In early 1942 the Japanese were incapable of invading Australia. The Japanese commitment to the land war in Southeast Asia was surprisingly modest. Its troops, though victorious in Malaya and Singapore, were easily outnumbered by the Allied defenders. In the whole southern land attack from December 1941 to May 1942, which included the Philippines, Burma, Malaya and Singapore, the Netherlands East Indies, New Britain, New Guinea and key US island mandates, the enemy committed only 200 000 troops. In the first half of 1942 the Japanese were in no position to invade Australia, and their relative position continued to deteriorate. By September 1942 the Allies had a force of 30 000 in New Guinea, for example. The Japanese had 10 000.

As military historian John Robertson concluded, Curtin tended 'somewhat to exaggerate the nature of the immediate threat facing Australia'. And as Australian historian Peter Stanley compellingly argues, there is little doubt he did so deliberately. MacArthur told the Advisory War Council on 26 March, five days after his arrival in Melbourne, that a Japanese invasion of Australia was unlikely because 'spoils here are not sufficient to warrant the risk'. Curtin himself acknowledged in Full Cabinet on 9 June that the 'Coral Sea and Midway Island battles had probably changed the Pacific strategic situation'. At the same Full Cabinet meeting he spoke of the future problem of demobilisation. Yet in September 1942, after the Coral Sea and Midway battles, at a time when Australia already had more than half a million men under arms and two American divisions were in Australia, Curtin was still pressing for an Allied force of 25 divisions for Australia's defence. That month he told reporters that the Japanese could base themselves in the Kimberleys and move overland 'diagonally across in this direction', a view which, as Stanley notes, contradicted both his advisers 'and common sense'. As late as March 1943 he was showing journalists a map supposedly detailing Japanese invasion plans, which he should have known and probably did know was not genuine. Curtin did not publicly concede that invasion was unlikely until June 1943 and it was not until September that he told Cabinet the danger of invasion had passed. Yet he would have been aware as early as April 1942 of Allied intelligence intercepts of Japanese communications showing that Japan did not plan to invade Australia.

It is certainly true that Curtin played up the threat of invasion. It may be, as one historian argues, that Curtin beat the invasion drum through 1942 and into 1943 to win advantage in the 21 August 1943 election. He had already conceded by then that invasion was unlikely, however, and there are more obvious motives for Curtin's earlier caution. He wanted to keep Parliament and public opinion focused on the threat of attack, because only by doing so could he evoke the co-operative spirit that made it possible both to mobilise Australia for war and to effect the changes to Australian institutions he believed would be required for peace. In England, Churchill also regretted that the danger of a German invasion of England had passed, for similar reasons.

Curtin had another and more powerful motive for stressing the Japanese threat and for demanding more ships and planes to meet it. His objective was to attack Japanese forces and defeat them, not merely to resist an invasion. He objected, as he said publicly on 26 January 1943, to a holding operation in the Southwest Pacific instead of a major counter-offensive. An invasion of Australia was, after all, merely the most vivid and calamitous threat presented by a Japanese presence that was anyway mortally dangerous. Even if Australia were not actually invaded, Japanese forces still controlled most of East Asia, Southeast Asia and the Southwest Pacific—the entire area Australia then and today regards as strategically significant.

Curtin might be confident that an invasion was unlikely, but in 1942 and into 1943 he could not be at all confident Japan would be forced to surrender all its conquests. The outcome of World War II and the political fortunes of Churchill and Roosevelt were entirely uncertain. The Afrika Korps under Rommel was poised to take Cairo until General Montgomery's offensive smashed through at El Alamein in October 1942. Marshall Zhukov's counter-attack on the German armies besieging Stalingrad did not begin until November 1942, and the battle was not over until February 1943. Through 1942 and into 1943 it remained possible that German armies would knock Russia out of the war, and the British out of the Middle East.

If the Soviet Union were crushed and the British driven out of the Middle East, it was also possible Churchill could be toppled by his opponents in the Conservative Party and Britain would reluctantly accept peace with Germany. That, after all, was Hitler's strategy, and Churchill had with difficulty fought off just such a peace plan in his own cabinet in May 1940. It was already evident that while Japan could not threaten the continental United States, it could be forced to a surrender only with great cost in American lives. It was exactly the position the Japanese military leadership hoped to achieve. No Australian prime minister could have excluded the risk that the United States and the United Kingdom might in some circumstances have agreed to a negotiated end to the war with Japan, in concert with peace in Europe, that would have left Japan the dominant East Asian and Southeast Asian military power. It was what Japan planned, and its military success had encouraged it to believe that outcome possible. So Curtin may have exaggerated the threat of invasion, but he did not exaggerate the threat Japan's regional domination then presented to Australia's freedom, independence and prosperity. His calls for more troops, more planes, more ships, for greater priority to the war in the Pacific, were intended not only to prevent the invasion of Australia, but also to prepare for the defeat of Japan.

Curtin's demands for greater resources for the Pacific war continued. Throughout the war in the Pacific he objected to the agreement between the United States and the United Kingdom to beat Germany first, which by implication meant that Japan would be contained to its 1942 conquests until Germany had surrendered. After Roosevelt and Churchill rejected his demands for more Pacific theatre aircraft at the Casablanca conference in January 1943, for example, Curtin protested in a radio address broadcast in England and America. The Southwest Pacific theatre, he said, 'is too crucial to be left to a force of caretakers'.

But while the priority accorded the war in Europe lingered on for decades as an Australian complaint against its wartime allies, in practice it made no difference to the war in the Pacific. American public opinion was so outraged by the Pearl Harbor attack that Roosevelt was compelled to give more support to the Pacific war than the formal agreement on priorities intended. The US Navy also lobbied for the Pacific theatre. Such was the immensity of US shipbuilding capacity that the Germany First strategy did not in fact slow the war against Japan by a day. As Bergerud writes, 'in the first year of the war more men and supplies went to the Pacific than were shipped to Europe', and 'the Navy throughout the war was able to procure far more resources for the Pacific' than the US supreme command planned. Indeed, through 1943 there were more US troops in the Pacific than in Europe. From 1942 to the end of the war the United States was able to build up its Pacific fleet much more rapidly than the Japanese could theirs. Australia's official Army war historian, Dudley McCarthy, came to the same conclusion, writing that while Roosevelt reiterated the Germany First policy to Curtin, in September 1942 there were more US troops overseas in the Pacific than the Atlantic. There were five divisions in the South and Southwest Pacific, and four in Hawaii compared with four in the overseas Atlantic. Almost all the US Naval Air Command was in the Pacific, as were 23 out of 57 US Army Air groups.

The drama of Australia's peril in February and March 1942 did not have a sequel that corresponded to the pattern of war in Europe. Despite Curtin's rhetoric, there never was a battle for Australia. Australia became an arsenal, a bread basket, a troops barracks and training ground for the assault by the American and Australian armies against Japanese power in the Pacific—just as Curtin had hoped. The Pacific War was not to be a conflict on land, however, but on sea and in the air. The Japanese Navy was checked in the battle of the Coral Sea as its troop transports approached Port Moresby in May 1942, and it was then crippled at the battle of Midway in June 1942. Australian troops stood firm against Japanese offensives in Papua in 1942, but if there was a saviour of Australia it was not Curtin or the Supreme Allied Commander in the Southwest Pacific, General MacArthur. It was US Pacific Naval commander Admiral Chester Nimitz, or perhaps more particularly Lieutenant Commander Wade McClusky of the carrier USS *Enterprise*, whose force of 37 Dauntless dive bombers flew off in the wrong direction, lost contact with its ship and, by astonishing luck, came on the Japanese fleet near Midway Island at 10.25 on the morning of 4 June 1942. The Japanese force had by then destroyed most of the US carrier planes and was preparing to sink the carriers as well. On the decks of their carriers were Japanese planes, refuelling in preparation for the final attack. Diving from 14 500 feet, McClusky's planes destroyed four Japanese aircraft carriers in an inferno of exploding aviation fuel, in five minutes reducing Japan from overwhelming superiority to bare parity with US carrier forces in the Pacific. It was, wrote John Keegan in his history of the war, 'the most stunning and decisive blow in the history of naval warfare' and one from which Japan would not recover.

US planes won the battle of Midway, though that battle was followed by a more intense and hard-fought battle on land as Japan pressed down the Solomons Islands group to Guadalcanal, and across Papua's Kokoda trail to Port Moresby. It was now forced on to the defensive, however, trying to secure its conquests. Within a year of Pearl Harbor Japan had lost control of the skies and the seas in the Pacific. Australian troops stopped the Japanese in Papua, but thereafter the naval and marine nature of the war meant Australian troops had only peripheral military importance in the war against Japan. Because the use of the atom bomb avoided an invasion of Japan, armies of any kind had limited military importance in its defeat. With the important exceptions of Burma, the Philippines and key islands in the US advance, on VJ day Japanese troops still held their land conquests which, with the loss of air and sea command, became just so many liabilities.

Because the war in the Pacific did not play out in massed land battles—unlike the war in Europe—and because Australian troops played only a very limited role in the defeat of Japan, Curtin never was and never could be a warlord like Churchill, Roosevelt, Stalin, Hitler, Tojo or Mussolini. He deliberately limited his own war role anyway, by placing the command of Australian forces under an American general, Douglas MacArthur, a decision for which he has since been criticised. The relationship worked well, writes Gavin Souter, 'only because Curtin looked after the rear, as he had been told, and left the front to the general', who had Curtin 'completely in his hands in military matters'.

It is true Curtin mostly went along with MacArthur in military matters, but in important respects Curtin's handling of the relationship with the US general was brilliant. Far from being imposed on Australia, Curtin, with the eager concurrence of War Cabinet, the Advisory War Council and military leaders, had sought an American commander of Allied forces in the region months before MacArthur turned up in Darwin in March 1942. Curtin wanted an American because that meant the United States was committed to defending Australia, and indeed Roosevelt's commitment to defend Australia and the appointment of MacArthur occurred on the same day. In the event, American Army troops were not decisive in 1942 or 1943 in the Southwest Pacific area and MacArthur's role as military commander in Australia was not as important as his role as a strategist, as a military adviser who could help Curtin interpret the war, and as a political ally of Curtin's both in pressing Australia's conversion to a war economy and in lobbying for more resources from Washington. With his direct access to the President discouraged (though not prevented) by Churchill, Curtin found the presence in Australia of one of the most brilliant, experienced, senior and politically fluent US commanders a considerable strength.

Under MacArthur, Australian General Thomas Blamey commanded both Australian and US troops in the land war in the Southwest Pacific area. He served under MacArthur, but as an American historian of the Pacific war writes, 'It is difficult to find a single instance where MacArthur asked the Australians to do something they themselves did not want to do'. In any case, 'the war in the Pacific was not a general's war' because most of the actions were so small in scale. Because it already had fighting experience, 'Australia had the best army in the South Pacific'. They arrived in Australia in increasing numbers, but American troops in the Southwest Pacific command were not important to the defence of Australia through 1942 or 1943. Indeed Blamey reported to Curtin at the end of 1942 that American troops 'cannot be classified as attack troops' and 'are definitely not equal to the Australian militia'. He wanted the 9th Division of the AIF brought back from the Middle East, and two US divisions given as substitutes. 'I do not think', he said of the US troops, 'they are a considerable addition to the defence of Australia'. As McCarthy wrote, 'Australians alone in the Southwest Pacific area faced the Japanese on land until November 1942'.

MacArthur's assumption of military command was first and foremost about the end of the military relationship with the United Kingdom. The transfer of command was not between an Australian general and MacArthur, but between Wavell as the former commander of the ABDA area and MacArthur as the Allied commander in the Southwest Pacific. Because he commanded all Allied troops on land, Blamey's command under MacArthur was far more substantial than his role under British command in the Middle East, or any Australian commander under Wavell. Curtin's insistence that the 7th come home was one symbol of Australia's changed relationship with the United Kingdom. A deeper and more permanent one was the removal of the Australian land forces from British command.

As historian Peter Edwards argues, MacArthur's presence in Australia was a direct link to the US high command it would not otherwise have had. Curtin had on hand a partner who knew Washington and its personalities, who had one of the finest strategic minds of the war and who shared Curtin's interest in winning additional resources for the Southwest Pacific. Since Curtin dealt directly with MacArthur, the relationship would have strengthened his position in Cabinet. Curtin was fortunate to have someone of MacArthur's quality close by, Shedden thought. He also recognised that when MacArthur left, Australia would again have to rely for knowledge of the higher direction of the war on its representatives in Washington and London. For Curtin, MacArthur supplied some of the insight into Washington which Churchill continued to obstruct, not least by persuading Australia's well-connected minister to Washington, Richard Casey, to accept a high-sounding British appointment in the Middle East—an appointment Churchill knew Casey would promptly accept.

In bringing the troops home, in insisting on the importance of the Pacific war, Curtin is often credited with turning away from the United Kingdom and forming the alliance with the United States that became the backbone of postwar Australian foreign policy. In his Melbourne *Herald* piece at the end of 1941 he wrote that Australia looked to America, free of any pangs as to the traditional links with the United Kingdom. But the central fact of the Pacific war was that Japan attacked the United States. It took Malaya for rubber and the Netherlands East Indies for oil, but the serious enemy was the United States—not Britain or the Netherlands colonial administration, and certainly not Australia. The United States and Australia were thus natural, instant, automatic and inevitable allies—rather more so in fact than the United States and the United Kingdom, had it not been for the good fortune of Hitler's prompt declaration of war on the United States. As MacArthur told Curtin in June 1942:

though the American people were animated by a warm friendship for Australia, their purpose in building up forces in the Commonwealth was not so much from an interest in Australia but rather from its utility as a base from which to hit Japan. In view of the strategical importance of Australia in a war with Japan, this course of military action would probably be followed irrespective of the American relationship to the people who might be occupying Australia.

There had never been any doubt that the United States rather than Britain would be Australia's major ally in a war with Japan. Churchill had said as much as First Sea Lord in March 1914, when he declared that 'If Great Britain's power were shattered the only course then open to the whites in the Pacific would be to seek the protection of the United States'. By the middle of 1941 it was a commonplace in Australian public discussion that America would be Australia's ally in a war with Japan. The dominant role for the United States in the Pacific was the basis of Allied planning in the area, and military co-operation between the United States and Australia was already well advanced when Japan attacked. Regional defence conferences including the United States and United Kingdom began in October 1940 and culminated in Washington talks between the two in January to March 1941. Australian defence officials were, for example, aware before the Pacific war began that the United States and the United Kingdom had already agreed that the war with Germany would have priority over the war with Japan if the United States entered the conflict. As early as October 1941 the Australian War Cabinet accepted a US proposal to strengthen the defences of Rabaul. Australia also discussed a US proposal for bases at Rabaul, Port Moresby, Rockhampton and Darwin to establish an air route between the Philippines and Hawaii. Just before the Japanese attack on Pearl Harbor, Shedden recounts, 'the United Kingdom Government informed the Australian Government that it had now received an assurance of the armed support of the United States' if Japan attacked Malaya or if the United Kingdom went to the support of the Netherlands East Indies.

The United Kingdom had long encouraged Australia to look to the United States as an ally in the Pacific, and for his part Curtin was much less willing to injure Australia's relationship with the United Kingdom than is often supposed. When Britain declared war on Germany in 1939, Menzies announced that since Britain was at war, Australia was also at war. Australia's own declaration of war against Japan in December is often cited as a measure of the independence of the Curtin government compared with Menzies. But while the terminology changed for Australia's declaration of war against Japan, the sense was not very different. At the Full Cabinet meeting hastily convened in Melbourne at 4.10 in the afternoon of 8 December it was explained (probably by Curtin, but perhaps by Evatt) that it was necessary 'to give authority to declare war at an appropriate time against Japan'. It would not be done that day because Congress had been summoned to meet on

8 December, 'subsequently to which the British proclamation will be made, and Australia will take action along similar lines to Great Britain'. Australians were already fighting the Japanese in Malaya, but Australia's declaration of war would await Great Britain's, which would await the Congress of the United States.

Curtin's conduct thereafter toward the United Kingdom and the United States was ambivalent. Australia under Curtin resisted US demands for a more liberal civil aviation policy and a more liberal trade policy, for example, and he pointedly told reporter Harold Cox that the British were making a very big contribution to the advance from Normandy in June 1944 though press reports made it appear the Americans did all the fighting. In speaking to conservative Adelaide voters during the 1943 election campaign, Don Rodgers recalled, Curtin wrapped himself in the Union Jack. When in London in 1944 he declared his belief in the British Empire, in the racial identity of Australians and Britons, and in Australia as a 'British community in the South Seas'.

Curtin got on very well indeed with the Governor General, Lord Gowrie. After the death of his son in combat in 1943, Gowrie wished to return to England. Long established Labor policy called for the appointment of an Australian Governor General, and indeed the first and hitherto only Australian appointment, Sir Isaac Isaacs, had been made by a Labor Prime Minister. Without referring the pending appointment to Cabinet Curtin decided to appoint the King's brother, the Duke of Gloucester, to the job. Not only was he British and an aristocrat, but also a member of the royal family. With the triumph of the 1943 election behind him, Curtin's political position was impregnable but even so Transport minister Eddie Ward was furious. Information minister Arthur Calwell also objected to the appointment. Ward complained in Cabinet in Canberra in November 1943 that he had learned of the appointment from the press. He asked why all ministers had not been advised of the appointment, and why it was made in opposition to the accepted policy of the Labor movement.

Defending the decision Curtin told his ministers that it was his view that all Government appointments were matters on which the Government in Cabinet had to come to a decision, but an appointment by the King was in another category. It was an appointment by the King on the advice of the Prime Minister. It was his 'personal duty to advise the King in such a matter', he told Ward, and 'the only adviser which the King or even the Governor General sees is the Prime Minister'. During the Cabinet debate Curtin believed or hoped—or perhaps merely found it convenient to assert—that a major British force might yet be sent to fight the Japanese in the Pacific, mentioning the possibility of British air, naval and perhaps land forces 'being stationed in Australia in the near future, and for a considerable period'. (Partly because the Pacific war circumstances did not require them, they did not arrive. But Curtin certainly wanted them, which showed he had not intended to turn his back on the United Kingdom when he turned toward the United States.) There was also another consideration. Like modern Australian monarchists, Curtin argued that members of the royal family were in some sense Australian as well as British. The 'Royal Family', he said, was 'the head of the whole Empire'. The King 'is as much the King of Australia as he is of the United Kingdom', he told Cabinet. He had 'very thoroughly' explored the option of appointing an Australian but could not 'settle upon a person who would be appropriate, who would have the necessary attributes of public service and of national distinction [and] who would not be associated with the military or some sectional interest'. Curtin discussed the association of Australia with both Britain and the United States, alluding to the policy of building existing links with the British while cultivating new ones with the United States.

Far from being anti-British Curtin was perhaps as close to the English point of view as Menzies, but it was a different England. As journalist Tom Fitzgerald pointed out in a 1977 lecture, Curtin's earliest mentors, Tom Mann and Frank Anstey, were both English born. Mann represented a tradition of English socialism that promoted worker education and stressed the importance of English literature as much as Marxist economics. Curtin was well read in Hardy, Meredith and Swinburne. When he thought of London he would have thought of the writers and the socialist politicians, where Menzies would have thought perhaps of the greatness of the common law tradition, of the English bar and the ruling class. There is a certain sense in which Menzies was more loyal to an Imperial idea than was Curtin. But there was also a sense in which both were loyal, though to different Englands. For Curtin that England was internationalist but not Imperial.

The reality of Curtin as warlord was very different from the legend. Bringing the troops home was the right decision to make, but it was not quite the decision of legend. The return was initiated by Churchill. Most of the AIF from the Middle East remained west of Singapore, until well into 1942 and Australia anyway had by March of that year a formidable military superiority over Japan's local forces should Japan have invaded—which it did not plan to do. Churchill did not let Australia down. The British fleet based on Singapore was around the size agreed in prewar planning and was satisfactory to Curtin just before the outbreak of war. The Malaya command was short of planes and tanks, but troop numbers were superior to those of the Japanese invaders. The fall of Singapore, which occurred around the same time and which was another source of resentment against Churchill, was important only because of the capture of Allied troops and particularly Australia's 8th Division—which would not have occurred if Australia had agreed to Churchill's wish to abandon its defence. Neither Curtin nor MacArthur nor Australian nor US Army troops had very much to do with putting Japan on the defensive in 1942, which was the result of US naval and marine victories under another command. Despite Australia's resentment the priority given to the war against Germany did not impair the war against Japan. Relinquishing command to MacArthur was a sensible decision, well managed by Curtin. But Curtin did not have much influence on high strategy, and indeed the war in the Pacific was not one that lent itself to high strategy.

If the war were all, one could conclude that Curtin's place in Australian history is on a spur to the main path. He stood up to Roosevelt and Churchill and saved Australians of the 7th Division from joining the 8th in Japanese prisoner-of-war camps, their almost certain fate had they been committed to Burma without air support or sea control, and under British command. He put Australia on a total war footing. He became the central figure in one of Australia's most affecting stories. But he did not fight the Battle of Australia because it never took place, and he did not 'save' Australia from a Japanese attack—which was always unlikely and soon impossible. He was not anti-British and could not be said to have created an alliance with the United States, which was the expected and inevitable outcome of war between Japan and America, and which was anyway a subsidiary aspect of the grander alliance between Roosevelt and Churchill. He did not take part in many of the key strategic decisions of the Pacific war. As a warlord Curtin was not in the class of Churchill or Roosevelt.

To see him in this diminishing way, however, is to miss the real Curtin story. His enduring importance does not lie in the war against Japan, but in how he was able to use the war against Japan to change the nature of Australian political institutions and Australia's economy. In our pursuit of military myths and national heroes, in the emotional trauma of Australia's separation from England, in our acceptance of his own posture as warlord, we have got Curtin seriously wrong.

5

Jack Curtin and the
Social Question

Curtin's sleepless vigil at the Lodge is one of the best remembered stories of early 1942, but it was not the only important event of that time. Within days of his appointment as Prime Minister on 7 October 1941 he had created the Production Executive with powers to determine what Australian factories and farms would produce and who they could employ. It initiated what Shedden later described as 'a feat without parallel in Australian history'. Resources and manpower were mobilised for the war effort. In mid-February 1942, at the same time as he was fighting with Churchill over the destination of the 7th Division, Curtin announced a National Economic Plan that made his Government the most powerful in Australian history, and himself its most powerful prime minister. Prompted by the urgency of the national crisis, shaped by the experience of the Depression and relying on powers available to the Commonwealth in war, Curtin would over the next three years refashion Australia's economic and political framework so completely and enduringly that much of his creation remains in place today.

To understand Curtin's motives and the ambition of his policy changes, we need first to understand the views, skills and analytical equipment he developed as a young man. Though his early career is best remembered for his opposition to conscription for overseas service during World War I, his central interest was in comprehending and transforming the economic world in which he found himself.

Born in Creswick, Victoria on 8 January 1885, Curtin came of age in a world that was becoming less kind to Australia than it had been. In the second half of the nineteenth century Australian workers enjoyed the highest living standards in the world. A small European population gifted with the laws and culture of England had been planted on a continent that proved to be both favourable for sheep and plentiful in gold. Through the nineteenth century Australia's population and its wealth doubled every few decades as it supplied this abundance to the world market. Australia in the nineteenth century sold a bigger share of its products in foreign markets and borrowed more overseas capital for the size of its economy than it would in the twentieth century.

Around the time of Curtin's birth, however, Australia's economic success was beginning to fade. Gold production declined and new grazing lands were less productive than existing grazing lands. In the early 1890s demand for wool, the principal export commodity, was checked by a downturn in the British economy. Prosperity in the 1880s had driven a land boom, with rapidly increasing bank lending and rising prices for pastoral and city land. As wool prices fell, some pastoralists were no longer able to meet their mortgages. Then as now most Australians were employed in service jobs in towns and cities, but they felt the pinch of declining rural prosperity. The speculative boom in property collapsed. In the early 1890s banks in Sydney and Melbourne began to fail. Between 1891 and 1893 five out of six banking businesses were forced to close, or to refuse payment to their depositors. It was 'the most severe shock ever experienced by the Australian financial system' and produced the demand for banking and currency reform that became Curtin's most important political battle.

With the financial system collapsing, the downturn became a depression. On the wharves and in the shearing sheds men formed unions and organised strikes that employers smashed in the long slump. The depression of the 1890s coincided with the rise of Labor parties, with the New South Wales Labor Party entering State Parliament in 1891. The establishment of a national bank was already a plank in its platform. Australia began to pick up again in the first decade of the new century, but the global economy on which Australia's success depended soon collapsed. The UK market remained and wartime needs saw commodity exports increase, but the free movement of capital, unhindered trade in goods and services and the global use of gold as the standard of wealth and payments all ended as European armies mobilised for war in 1914.

As a child Curtin would have seen some of the distress of the crash of the 1890s. He was the eldest of four children of Irish immigrants. His father was a policeman who left the service to become a hotel manager in Melbourne. In poor health, he was not a successful publican and the family moved from hotel to hotel, with each new hotel usually a little shabbier than the last. The family eventually settled in Brunswick, where the young Curtin played cricket and football and performed reasonably but not exceptionally at school. Like most working-class boys he left school at 14, in 1900, the year before the six colonies federated into a nation. The young Curtin found work as a copyboy, a page at a club and in the printing and pottery industries before settling down for seven years as estimates clerk with a company that manufactured nails and other hardware. It was a job he could soon handle easily, one that gave him some autonomy as a skilled specialist, and in which he acquired a fluency in mental arithmetic that would astound colleagues in coming decades.

Curtin spent his childhood and early adult years in a turbulent, disappointing economic world. As a result, from his earliest writing and speaking, Curtin's principal preoccupation was what he sometimes referred to as the Social Question, and we would now call economics. Socialism is above all an economic theory, and Curtin held it passionately in his early adult life. From his earliest surviving letters we know the restless quality of his intellect and the breadth of his reading. He stocked his mind with the poetry and novels of late nineteenth century England and with socialist texts. Even among working-class socialists, who read more than today's professional politicians, he was unusually well read and thoughtful. As a Member of Parliament he would say that while he did not believe in compulsory military training, compulsory unionism or compulsory voting he did believe in compulsory education. Through frequent speeches, the demands of political conflict and of propaganda he assimilated and constantly reworked his material, and his views were subject to frequent criticism and discussion. There is little doubt that by the time he reached Federal Parliament he had a stronger command over economic analysis than all but a few of his contemporaries. He was certainly better grounded and more widely read in economic analysis than Menzies or Labor's wartime treasurer Ben Chifley, and perhaps than any other member except Labor's treasurer during the Depression, Ted Theodore.

Central to understanding his conduct in government is the development of the views he brought to office in 1941 from his earliest adulthood in Melbourne.

The young Curtin was active in the Victorian Socialist Party (VSP) by 1905 and soon became a formidable polemicist. Under the influence of British socialist Tom Mann, who lived in Australia from 1902 to 1909, the VSP focused on education and propaganda. It was Marxist in economic outlook, believing not only that socialist equality was a morally better system but that capitalism contained internal contradictions that would eventually destroy it. The viewpoint and content was economic analysis rather than idealism. Its adherents, which then included Curtin, thought of socialism not so much as a faith, value or political preference, but as a social science. Curtin was to say in a speech long after that 'the Labor movement, scientifically viewed, is not an uprising for the redress of grievances, but the desire that correct economic laws shall prevail'.

By 21 Curtin was thinking about Australia's part in a system of global capitalism that he believed relentlessly increased production while forcing down wages. Writing in September 1906 in the VSP paper *The Socialist* on 'The International Spirit', Curtin asserted that in Australia, as elsewhere, 'the volume of trade is ever increasing, the development of industry and commerce is continuous in its march towards perfection in method and finality in possibility, yet millions starve, in all countries—whether Europe, America or Africa, whether protectionist or free trade, whether republic or monarchy. This is why the plutocrats resist the extensions of democracy.'

Though he may not have read the originals, Curtin was able to base his views not only on Karl Marx but also on the two great classical economists, Adam Smith and David Ricardo. Writing in *The Socialist* around the time of his twenty-second birthday he recalled that 'During what I may call the time when I first realized the necessity of obtaining some knowledge of the Social Question, I came across two statements which have firmly implanted themselves in my mind'. One was a statement of Adam Smith that 'the produce of labour constituted the natural recompense or wages of labour'. The other was a statement by Ricardo that 'labour is like unto any other commodity, in so much as its value is determined by its cost of production, and that the cost of production is the cost of the labourer's subsistence'. Together the two statements suggested to Curtin that labour is the source of all value, but the labourer is not paid more than a subsistence income. He referred to Lassalle, who called this 'the iron and cruel law of wages', and to Marx, to whom he attributed the view that as productivity of labour rises the cost of maintaining labour falls. The root of it all is a system of production for profit based on individual competition. It was inherent in capitalism, he thought, that wage income would not keep up with production. The essence of the Social Question, he concluded, is that the power of production exceeds the power of consumption.

The under-consumptionist view he formed at 22 would remain an important piece of his thinking, particularly when Australia slid into the Great Depression a quarter of a century later. Within a few years his explanation of the gap between production and consumption would extend to include the role of banks and the international role of the gold standard. It would lead directly to his quick sympathy for the English economist Maynard Keynes and to his early understanding of both the forces at work during the Depression, and some possible remedies. A decade later it would motivate changes to the whole economic framework of the Australian Commonwealth.

In the VSP Curtin found an intellectual and emotional home. By February 1907 *The Socialist* was advertising Curtin as a 'conductor' in an Elocution and Economics class, meeting in the Socialist Party Hall, Elizabeth Street, Melbourne every Tuesday. Teaching as well as reading, Curtin would have been forced to master the material rather than merely browsing it. Three years later he was a regular lecturer on economic issues. In a speech reported in July 1910 he declared that 'economic knowledge [was] the supreme need'.

Curtin was deeply influenced by the VSP leader Tom Mann and throughout his life would be drawn to an England that was for him the poetry and novels of the English humanist tradition, and to British socialism. Mann was an internationalist, so he brought to the VSP and to Curtin a way of placing Australia in the context of global capitalism and world events. He was a propagandist, and part of his legacy was an emphasis on education rather than organisation and political struggle. He was well read in literature, and like many British socialists of his time he thought good poetry, plays and novels would enlighten and uplift the working class.

By the time Mann left in 1909, Curtin had come to know him well. Speaking at Mann's farewell in the upstairs dining room of the Rubira Café in Bourke Street, Curtin proposed the toast of 'The Social Revolution'. He told the 130 guests that 'Tom Mann's greatness . . . consisted in ever keeping in view the big thing, and yet not being negligent of the small things'. (Mann's racial views did not have such a lasting impact, though they were noted. Another speaker told the farewell that 'Mr Mann was the first public man he had heard say a word for the Italians, and other races than the white'.)

Mann's last message in *The Socialist* on Christmas Eve 1909 was that 'the work of the Socialist Party must be primarily EDUCATIONAL'. He also supported industrial unionism, as opposed to a strategy of winning power through parliaments. 'Don't spend time denouncing Parliaments', he advised, 'but do spend time showing that real economic power rests in the hands of those workers who actually engage in the making of useful things and the doing of useful things . . .'. He thought his Australian comrades should be glad of the opportunity to do some of the work of overthrowing capitalism and establishing socialism, to be part of the 'great and ever increasing struggle to cast down Mammon and Greed and establish the people on a basis of universal love and good will'. Following Mann, Curtin remained a committed socialist before World War I, sceptical of the Labor Party. *The Socialist* of 22 July 1910 reported a speech by Curtin claiming that everywhere 'productive power was in excess of consumptive power'. The Labor Government would be in a bad way in a few years' time, 'when it realized that monopoly could not be ended as it prescribed, and unemployment was rife'. The only solution was 'social ownership'.

Curtin admired Mann, but the most important mentor in his political career was another Englishman, Frank Anstey. After Anstey's death, Curtin would say that:

> of all the men who have influenced me, he influenced me the most. He introduced me to the Labour movement. He set my mind going in the direction he wished it to go, and in quite a humble way I sought to play the role of a supporter, an aider, an abettor to the cause to which he had introduced me, believing it to be the greatest cause in the world. The longer I have lived, the more truth have I discovered in the urgings he gave to me.

Born to poor parents in London in 1865, at the age of eleven Anstey stowed away on a passenger vessel bound for Sydney. He spent the following decade as a seaman from Australian ports, sailing to the South Pacific and Asia. Marrying and moving to Melbourne in the 1890s, Anstey was drawn into the ferment of left-wing political movements that accompanied the rise of the Labor Party. He himself did not join Mann's VSL, but spoke at its meetings. He was the moving spirit of the Brunswick Labor Party, and from 1902 the member for East Bourke in State Parliament. In 1910 Anstey became Member of the House of Representatives for Bourke. Curtin became a member of the Brunswick Labor Party, and went along on Sunday mornings to join a discussion group that met at Anstey's home. In March 1907 Curtin was elected President of Anstey's Brunswick branch of the Political Labor Council. Curtin chaired meetings for Anstey during the 1907 Victorian State election. Curtin's first biographer, Lloyd Ross, believed even Curtin's speaking style was influenced by Anstey, who was one of the most powerful orators of his day. Anstey drew Curtin into electoral politics by urging him to stand for the safe Liberal seat of Balaclava in the 1914 Federal election. When he slipped into heavy drinking, Anstey helped him recover. Anstey's lifelong cause was the public ownership of banking, and his lifelong conviction was that the world's workers were exploited by those who controlled the levers in the global financial system. Curtin would later publish excerpts from his 1917 book, *The Kingdom of Shylock*, in the *Westralian Worker*. Anstey thought high finance responsible for the world's ills, and that its secret manipulators were mostly Jews. His cranky monetary views had a lingering influence on Curtin. Anstey was a strong supporter of the foundation of the Commonwealth Bank by the Fisher Government in 1911, and later a strong opponent of conscription for service in World War I. Curtin shared these causes. Anstey would later be Curtin's colleague in Federal Parliament during the Depression years.

Anstey was twenty years older than Curtin. Of those in his own generation Frank Hyett was the most important influence. Born a few years earlier than Curtin and like him an early member of the VSP, Hyett was the better cricketer and, when they first met, more advanced in economics. In a piece Curtin wrote after Hyett's death in 1919 at 37, he recalled that he had first met Hyett about fifteen or sixteen years earlier in Brunswick. Curtin had been handed the telegram announcing Hyett's death while in a union meeting. 'I will not forget that day if I live to be 90', he wrote. 'Ever since I have been living again old days. The Socialist Party in Collins Street; meetings here, there and everywhere; football and cricket matches; card games we played, and all the little things and big things that have made up fifteen years of intimacies about almost everything, and which became part of ourselves as we grew from youth on.' Hyett was evidently the first source of his education in economics. Curtin recalled that, 'Frank had then read a good deal of economics—I was a blank. Somehow, I think he filled me up. For I do not know ever subsequently differing from him on the view he took towards the things to do and way to do them'. This would date Curtin's reading and thinking about economics as starting from around the age of eighteen or nineteen.

From his job as a price estimator Curtin moved on in 1911 to become Secretary of the Victoria Timber Workers' Union, a job that required him to prepare material about wages and working conditions to State wages boards, and to oversee the preparation of union accounts. By the time he left Melbourne in 1917 he was thus not only well read in contemporary and classical economic theory, but also practised in the basic skills of public business. He was good at arithmetic, he would have known something about accounting and he would have had a good understanding of wages and working conditions and the style of argument before arbitration tribunals. Because of his induction to economic analysis through Mann and the VSP, Curtin's natural perspective was international rather than local. He was always aware of the global causes of local economic troubles.

Troubled by alcoholism and the timber workers' profound lack of interest in socialist revolution, he left the union after four years. At 30 he was drinking heavily and only sporadically employed. He fought in the anti-overseas conscription campaign of 1916, but Melbourne was no longer congenial. Anstey encouraged Curtin to apply for the editorship of the *Westralian Worker*, the Labor Party newspaper of Western Australia. Anstey also did everything he could to make sure he was offered the job. He wrote a reference for Curtin, lobbied prominent members of the Western Australian Labor Party, and went to Perth to urge the merits of his candidate in January 1917, when the decision was being made. When Curtin got the job Anstey advised him on how to run the paper, and contributed many articles in the early days of Curtin's editorship.

Curtin welcomed the chance to make a fresh start. He sailed from Melbourne to Perth in February 1917, aged 32. Escaping persistent and increasing drunkenness he left the biggest city in Australia, left his life there as one of its best-known Labor leaders and a principal opponent of conscription, and left his friends and colleagues of fifteen years of socialist agitation, for marriage, fatherhood and a new life in the tiny, remote Indian Ocean capital of Western Australia. Rounding the Great Australian Bight on board the *Katoomba* he wrote to Western Australian Labor leader Hugh Mahon, who had supported him for the new job despite his alcohol addiction, a letter of extraordinary candour and humility.

> It is quite impossible for me to ever thank you sufficiently for having so generously given me this chance to be useful to the world and to myself. I was prepared for rebuff and a long and heavy road but to some extent the worst is past. I shall do my best to vindicate your confidence. More than anything I shall strive to justify in that respect which has to do with my personal conduct . . . Thank you very sincerely and may the sequel demonstrate that I stick firm in the upward path you were good enough to assist me to commence.

Marrying Elsie Needham, the daughter of a socialist painter and signwriter then living in Tasmania, he built a new life in Perth and began to play an increasingly prominent role in Western Australian Labor politics.

Curtin edited the *Westralian Worker* for the next twelve years. There for the first time he exposed himself to economic training in a non-socialist environment by attending external courses offered by Edward Shann, Professor of History and Economics at the University of Western Australia in Perth. Shann was a neo-classical economist and in favour of the gold standard, which Curtin opposed. He was also a vocal critic of what he called 'hermit economy' policies, arguing that increasing tariff protection for Australian manufacturing industry was at the expense of higher costs for farm industries. There was not much manufacturing industry in Western Australia, which in the national debate usually supported free trade against Victoria's protectionism. Curtin's vigorous support of high tariffs may have faded as a result of his contact with Shann and the circumstances of Western Australia. At all events he was later only a moderate protectionist, in contrast with some of his Labor colleagues. Shann's belief in self-regulating capitalism had little impact on Curtin, not least because the Great War was followed by a deep global recession. 'No corresponding improvement has fallen to the worker's lot as a consequence of the mechanical improvements' in the past century in the United States and United Kingdom, he told a Perth audience the year after the war ended. 'Production for profit leads to over-production', he said, 'and over-production inevitably leads to unemployment'. He believed 'the capitalist system is collapsing'. Over the years in Perth, however, his views moderated. One influence was his reading.

One often repeated view would later be the key to his achievement. He frequently pointed to the contrast between what capitalist governments were able to do in war, and what they claimed was impossible in peace. It followed that war could be seen as a good time to make revolutionary changes. In a June 1917 speech Curtin said:

Governments which could raise millions for the prosecution of this fearful war by merely lifting their little finger, when confronted with the problem of saving from semi-starvation the many millions of their people existing in abject poverty could do nothing but unearth reports from pigeon holes to prove their utter inability to improve the situation of the people.

Curtin's wide reading continued in Perth. As editor and chief writer for the paper he read and reviewed many newly published works on economics. His favourite economist now was not Marx or Ricardo but Maynard Keynes, who was beginning the intellectual journey that would lead him to his 1936 *General Theory of Employment, Interest and Money* and the destruction of many of the tenets of orthodox theory. Soaking up the new books, Curtin himself was beginning his own intellectual journey from Marxist economics to the liberal and interventionist market economy views of Keynes. Curtin had evidently read Keynes' *A Revision of the Treaty*, *Tract on Monetary Reform* and *Economic Consequences of the Peace* by 1924. He would later write that 'there is no more interesting person in the world of economics' than Keynes.

He continued to speak as well as to write, and he had a useful opportunity to study one issue in detail in 1927 and 1928 as a Labor member of a Royal Commission appointed by the Bruce–Page Government to report on child endowment. By the end of the 1920s Curtin had established himself as one of the most skilled economic analysts on the left in Australia. He was certainly not academically trained, and Frank Anstey's confused monetary views confused Curtin as well. But he had an excellent understanding of contemporary economic thought and of the state of the world economy. This accumulation of knowledge was about to be tested by two events—Curtin's election to Federal Parliament, and the beginning of the Great Depression.

6

Jack Curtin MHR and the Great Depression

With almost three decades of engagement in the economic debate behind him, Curtin was elected to Federal Parliament as the Labor Member for the seat of Fremantle in the general election of 1928. He was now on the national stage, but the coming three years would prove difficult—for Australia, for the Labor Party and for Curtin himself.

The following year Labor won a majority in the House of Representatives, and Government in a general election that saw Prime Minister Stanley Bruce lose his seat. Labor leader Jim Scullin became Prime Minister. In the Federal Labor Caucus Curtin was reunited with his mentor, Frank Anstey, who had been Deputy Leader of the parliamentary party from 1922 to 1927, a year before Scullin was elected leader. Though Curtin was now in his early forties and on the executive of the federal Caucus, though long associated with the Labor Party and an effective orator, he was denied election to the Scullin ministry. He lost the ballot partly because of his drinking, and because he was junior to the other Western Australian MP who was elected to the ministry. But it didn't help that Curtin was also a close friend of Anstey, who was disliked by the brilliant Labor Party Deputy Leader and Treasurer, former Queensland Premier and now NSW Member of the House of Representatives, Ted Theodore. Curtin saw Theodore as 'the chief figure in defeating me in the party' and a reporter who spent much time with Curtin later wrote that rightly or wrongly, Curtin believed Theodore had kept him out of the ministry. It would be another two years before Curtin moved closer to Theodore than to Anstey.

Born in Port Adelaide in 1884 Theodore left school at 12, working as a gardener and timber-getter before moving to the Western Australian goldfields and then to the mines at Broken Hill. In his early twenties he formed a labour union in North Queensland and became its secretary. He became a member of the Queensland Legislative Assembly in 1909, Deputy Premier and Treasurer in 1915 and Premier at the age of 35 in 1919. Like Curtin he had left school early and read widely, developed his political skills in the trade union movement, and fought against Prime Minister Billy Hughes' conscription referendums in 1916 and 1917. Offered the NSW seat of Dalley in 1927 after failing to be elected in 1925 for the Queensland seat of Herbert, Theodore supported Scullin for the party leadership in 1928 and became Deputy Leader in February 1929. When Labor won office in October 1929 he became Deputy Prime Minister. 'Carefully attired', writes one of his biographers, 'aloof, grave and measured in manner, the new treasurer stood out in a parliament where his air of brooding strength and confident grasp of the world at large intimidated colleague and foe alike'.

Labor's victory on 12 October 1929 coincided with a deepening global depression. Wall Street crashed soon after Labor won Government, but in Australia wheat and wool prices had been falling for several years as global demand for commodities fell. The economy was already contracting and unemployment was rising. Within a few years there would be more than half a million unemployed, or by some estimates almost one third of the male workforce. Divided by class antagonisms, fearful of both red revolution and fascism, 'armed forces paraded in the open and organised in secret'. It would be another three years before Australians saw the first glimmer of hope for recovery.

The Depression struck Australia early because the nation depended on wool and wheat exports, and with all the more severity because it followed a decade of high government development spending financed by foreign borrowing. Through the 1920s Australian governments invested heavily in roads, railways, bridges, ports and other public works to sustain a rapidly growing economy and an increasing population. National debt had doubled, and half of it was owed to foreign creditors—principally in London. The government interest bill to foreign creditors was fixed, but tax revenue was falling and unemployment was rising rapidly. When the Depression hit, the London loans dried up. In the three years to 1930–31 annual capital inflow averaged £49 million. In the following three years there was a net outflow. In 1929 the balance of payments deficit had swollen to more than a tenth of GDP. In the following two years imports fell by two thirds. Unable to pay the money back, the Federal Government needed to roll over the existing loans. To pay the bills as tax revenue fell and spending increased, the government needed to continue borrowing.

The new Government depended on the goodwill of the London financial community and the Australian banks. But Scullin and Theodore could not demand the co-operation of even the Government-owned Commonwealth Bank. Created by the Government of Labor Prime Minister Andrew Fisher in 1911, the Commonwealth Bank was designed to address some of the problems evident in the banking collapse of the 1890s. It would be able to support other banks in temporary difficulties, and also lend to business and households at times when private banks were reluctant to do so. The 1911 legislation did not confer central banking functions, however, not least because the theory and practice of central banking were then in their infancy. Under the Fisher legislation the bank was directed by a governor appointed by the Treasurer for a term of seven years. In 1924 a Nationalist Coalition Government led by Stanley Bruce and Earle Page amended the Act to put the Bank under the control of a board appointed by the Government. Though the Bill was said to confer central banking powers on the Bank it did not do so except in respect of the issue of money. Control of the note issue was transferred from a Notes Board to the Bank. By 1929 the Bank was under the firm control of the business community through its board, and protected by legislation from direction by the Treasurer. It had not the least hesitation in asserting itself. Meeting Cabinet soon after Labor took office on 22 October 1929, Commonwealth Bank chairman Sir Robert Gibson told the assembled ministers the Bank was entirely independent and he would accept neither advice nor requests from the Scullin Government. He would give Scullin and Theodore another five weeks to show how spending would be cut to reduce the growing government deficit. Unless he was satisfied, the Bank would not finance the Commonwealth beyond the end of November.

Pressed by creditors in London and by the banks in Australia, the Scullin Government also faced a hostile Senate that rejected legislation to establish government control over banking. The new Government was able to raise tariffs at the end of 1929, and it cut back on assisted immigration to Australia. Thereafter its plans to deal with the Depression were blocked by the Senate or the Commonwealth Bank.

The strains that destroyed the Scullin Government over the next three years arose from the conflict between rising social spending, fixed interest payments, falling government income and the need for support from the Australian banks and London creditors. Following orthodox theory, the bankers and most economists insisted that Australia must respond to the downturn by cutting government spending to reduce or eliminate deficits. Governments could cut spending by cutting the wages of their employees, by sacking government workers, and by minimising depression relief. Orthodoxy also urged cutting wages generally, both because falling prices meant after-inflation wage incomes had increased and because lower wages would allow employers to hire more workers. The problem with the orthodox prescription—a problem readily recognised within the Labor Caucus—was that as incomes were cut, spending fell and the Depression deepened. It was not until Keynes' *General Theory* appeared in 1936 that there was a satisfactory economic rationale to justify it, but in most countries (including Australia) revenues fell much faster than spending, and government deficits increased.

Labor's plans were blocked, and the Party was soon divided. From April 1930 to March the following year, journalist Warren Denning wrote, 'Party meetings were a bedlam and sometimes a riot'. Troubled by the Depression, saddened by the Scullin Government's inability to get its own program through, indignant at the policies of retrenchment it was obliged to adopt instead, with no ministerial duties and a long train journey away from his family in Perth, Curtin drank and talked late into the night with other morose colleagues. He also became one of the party's most eloquent and trenchant analysts of the long slump. In those three otherwise lost years he adopted and expounded some of the major policies he would implement as Prime Minister a decade later.

Throughout Australia debate raged over the slump. Mainstream economists argued over the size of a tolerable deficit, the nature of tax increases and spending cuts, and whether it was useful to depreciate the Australian pound against the English pound. The result of their discussions was a series of three Economists' Plans for Depression. The Commonwealth Bank had its own policy prescription, which insisted on governments working toward balanced budgets in exchange for the Bank supporting the payment of interest on loans in London. The Bank's view was supported and encouraged by Bank of England representative Sir Otto Niemeyer, who visited Australia in 1930 and proposed action along similar lines. NSW Labor Premier Jack Lang took a more radical stance, arguing that payments of interest on the State and Federal Government bonds should be suspended.

To Curtin the problem centred on the control of credit. The global and Australian depressions had been created, he thought, partly because the international gold standard restricted the growth of credit, and production outran demand. If the banks expanded credit in Australia by making loans cheaper and more widely available, demand would begin to increase. In a 6 December 1929 speech during the Budget debate, Curtin quoted Australian economist Douglas Copland, later to be one of his Prime

Ministerial advisers, to the effect that 'the major cause of unemployment is to be found in banking and credit policies'. This would remain the central theme of Curtin's analysis of the Depression. Six months later, for example, he spoke in support of the Government's Central Reserve Bank Bill, which proposed the establishment of a Reserve Bank separate from the Commonwealth Bank. The Bill would have given the Government authority to instruct the Commonwealth Bank, a power it would certainly use to raise more loans from the Bank. It was, as expected, defeated by the Opposition in the Senate.

As the crisis deepened, Curtin's analysis became more wide-ranging. In 1930 he published *Australia's Economic Crisis and the £55,000,000 Interest Bill*, a pamphlet presenting his analysis of the causes of the Depression and its remedies. He portrayed the problem as one of insufficient demand, which he saw primarily as a shortage of credit. The analysis is obscured by a tangled account of the role of interest payments on bonds, an instance of the crank monetary theories Curtin shared with Anstey. But it did rightly identify the gold standard as a constraint on credit creation, and Curtin was far ahead of most of his contemporaries in going a remarkably big step further and advocating depreciation of the Australian pound against the pound sterling.

Depreciation of the Australian pound was resisted by the banks, not least because it would increase the cost of interest payments on debt in sterling. To economists schooled in the gold standard it threatened competitive devaluations, in which the advantages of depreciation were lost when other countries did the same. Even Keynes opposed depreciation of the Australian pound, arguing in a comment commissioned for the Melbourne *Herald* that it was not as effective as public spending, and could be matched by devaluation elsewhere. For Australian exporters of wheat and wool, however, and for Australian manufacturers who competed against foreign-made products, depreciation made a lot of sense. The farmers would be paid more in Australian pounds. The manufacturers would be more competitive against imports. Curtin's support of depreciation, which soon extended to arguing that demand and supply should set the exchange rate for the Australian pound, was an early instance of his willingness to impose an Australian perspective and to refuse an English perspective on Australia—even when the English perspective was that of that most interesting economist, Keynes.

In early July 1930 Theodore was forced to step down as Treasurer after the Queensland Government released the report of a Royal Commission that accused him of benefiting from government mining transactions while in government in Queensland. On 18 August Niemeyer proposed to a Premiers' Conference in Melbourne a program of cost cutting and budget balancing for the States and the Commonwealth. This became the core of the 21 August Melbourne Agreement between the States and the Commonwealth. At the end of August an exhausted Scullin began what became a six-month visit to England, hoping by personal contact to reassure London creditors.

While in London he remained both Prime Minister and Treasurer, communicating by cable with Acting Prime Minister James Fenton and Acting Treasurer Joe Lyons. These two leaders, neither of whom had the intellectual force of Theodore or the party command of Scullin, attempted to hold together a deeply divided Government. Backed up by Scullin, who lost touch with the rapid radicalisation of Caucus as the economic crisis deepened, Lyons tried to implement the Melbourne Agreement. He argued that the Government had little choice but to remain in office, implementing spending cuts and reassuring the banks. The leader of NSW Premier Jack Lang's supporters in Federal Parliament, Jack Beasley, argued that foreign creditors should share the pain by being denied interest payments. Anstey, Curtin and their allies argued that the Government should force a double dissolution of Parliament and go to the people with a Labor program for recovery. If it lost, the Opposition should bear responsibility for implementing the policies now forced on the Government by the Commonwealth Bank and the conservative majority in the Senate. From the backbench Theodore and his allies sought a middle ground that would see reduced deficits over a longer period.

In the leadership vacuum created by the absence of Scullin, Curtin became a leading Caucus critic.

Though a minister in the Scullin Government, Anstey strongly disagreed with the strategy of remaining in office while the Opposition-controlled Senate rejected Scullin's attempts to gain control over banking. Anstey wanted to force a double dissolution, arguing that Labor in government was being blamed for what it was prevented from remedying. This was also Curtin's view. But while he shared that view with Curtin and Theodore did not, Anstey was well to the left of both Curtin and Theodore in his support for bank nationalisation, and ultimately in his preference for Lang's policies over those of Scullin.

Curtin was an early and vigorous opponent of a policy of spending cuts, wage reductions and tax increases. The morning after Niemeyer addressed State and Federal Government representatives meeting as the Loan Council on the need to cut spending, Curtin moved in Caucus that the Treasurer make a 'full and frank statement of the Financial Position of Australia, [and] that Party have a full discussion' the following day. That motion was lost, but Caucus was breaking up into a radical Lang faction, supporters of Lyons, and a group led by Anstey that included Curtin.

Theodore returned to the Caucus debate in October, as Lyons brought forward proposals to implement the Melbourne Agreement. Caucus resistance was increasing. On the afternoon of 27 October Jack Beasley successfully moved a motion rejecting the 'Tariff and Industrial Policy' proposed by Niemeyer at the Melbourne Premiers' Conference. The Caucus debate continued the next day, with Lyons proposing an apparently radical policy that depended, however, on the willingness of the Commonwealth Bank to implement it. Lyons moved that the policy of the party should be: '(1) Free exchange rates

(2) stabilisation of internal prices by monetary control
(3) reduction of interest rates (4) provision of credits for
industry—and that every effort shall be made by the
Government to induce the Commonwealth Bank to carry
out such a policy'. An amendment moved by NSW member
G.A. Gibbons and seconded by Theodore required the
Commonwealth Bank to create sufficient credit for the
purposes of the Government. It specified a fixed exchange
rate, though by implication the rate would be markedly
lower. The amendment was carried the following day,
leaving Lyons as acting Treasurer with a Caucus instruction
to require the Commonwealth Bank to provide sufficient
credit to meet all the budgetary needs of the
Commonwealth, and all maturing internal loans. There was
of course no prospect of the Commonwealth Bank agreeing
or of Lyons asking it to. From London Scullin backed
Lyons. On 6 November Anstey and Curtin saw an opportunity to force a confrontation with the Commonwealth
Bank, proposing a Caucus resolution that the Bank be
required to take over a Commonwealth loan about to fall
due. The motion was passed, but Lyons again called in
Scullin's support and on this occasion Theodore also
backed Lyons.

On 12 November Curtin offered his most penetrating
criticism of Depression remedies, including those of the
Labor Government. The previous week Lyons had proposed
a financial statement cutting Commonwealth Government
spending. The statement followed the visit of Niemeyer
and a subsequent August agreement by the Commonwealth

and the State Premiers to balance their budgets for the 1930–31 financial year. In language Keynes might have used, Curtin argued that by reducing demand every spending cut made the depression deeper and the deficits bigger. Every 'step they take along the road of the Niemeyer plan makes it increasingly difficult' for State and Federal governments to balance their budgets. Every 'reduction in wages, every rationing of employment, every diminution in the purchasing power of the community, reacts upon the taxpaying capacity, and as a result the revenues which have been forecast by the Treasurers, Commonwealth or State, have not been, and will not be, realized'.

The Opposition bore a great deal of responsibility because it had accumulated during the 1920s the foreign debt on which interest must then be paid. 'If to fail to pay one's way each year is a cardinal offence against national honour', he said, 'the Labor Party is not the initiator of this chapter of obloquy in the national history. It has been written by others in circumstances less justifiable than the present'. But the Government's direction was now wrong: Australia's problem was part of a world problem—that the productive power had 'greatly outstripped the means of exchange'. Niemeyer's prescription meant deflation of all incomes except those derived from investments in government stocks. In his support he instanced 'Mr J.M. Keynes in his *The Economic Reconstruction of Europe*', where it was argued that 'there comes a point when the problem of meeting the national debt is insoluble by orthodox methods'.

Curtin instead urged credit creation or an expansion of the money supply, a response to the Depression that would then or later be approved by both Milton Friedman and the monetarists, and Keynes and the Keynesians, and today by the US Federal Reserve and the Bank of Japan, and by the International Monetary Fund. Curtin quoted Australian economist E.C. Dyason in favour of 'greater monetary stability', pointing to the support Dyason found in the views of Keynes. ('Monetary stability' in the half century following World War II meant arresting *inflation*. In the Depression it meant arresting *deflation* or falling prices, a sense it regained when deflation once again became a threat early in the twenty-first century.) He approvingly quoted Dyason's claim of a program of additional credit creation that, 'The Board of the Commonwealth Bank can adopt it tomorrow and, probably, cure within a reasonable time (say two years) half, but not the whole of our present ills'.

But Curtin went further and argued for a flexible exchange rate, a policy that would not become orthodox for another 40 years and would not be implemented in Australia until the dollar was floated by Labor Prime Minister Bob Hawke and Treasurer Paul Keating in December 1983.

I would ask this Parliament to consider the undesirability of allowing the banks to peg the rate of exchange at whatever figure they care to choose. To begin with, the pegging of exchange rates by banks in Australia has not been done in the interests of Australia, but has been resorted to simply as a measure of protection by each of the banks in order to prevent competition in regard to their transactions . . . they have arbitrarily pegged the rate of exchange at a figure which does not square with the ordinary operations of supply and demand.

Curtin suggested three measures that, translated into contemporary terminology, all became orthodoxy and all of which were then rejected by the Australian banks, many economists and by the Opposition. The first was a floating exchange rate: 'the banks should be compelled to unpeg the exchange and allow it to operate naturally'. The second was to allow a budget deficit to persist for longer by reducing it more gradually. He wanted a three- or five-year plan rather than a one-year plan to restore 'financial equilibrium' or a balanced budget. And, finally, he wanted an expansion of what today would be called lending or credit or the money supply. The board of the Commonwealth Bank, he said, should 'restore the note issue to the per capita requirements of the Australian people'. He claimed the note issue was then £7 per head compared with the previous level of £9 per head. This 'deliberate contraction' of the note issue had been one of the problems. He explained that increasing the note issue went hand in hand with increased lending. There should be 'requisite accommodation' for farmers and small business.

The central problem with all three policies, and one that would remain in the forefront of his thinking, was that

'As a result of legislation passed by the previous Government, this Government has no power over the monetary policy of Australia, and cannot interfere with its banking policy'. He also evoked the contrast between war and peace that had so forcefully struck him during the Great War, and which would be at the centre of his thinking during World War II. If war broke out next week or next month, he argued, those controlling the banks and financial institutions 'would be able to finance the frightful tragedy of an international war with all the celerity which, in the history of a nation, marks the black magic of money power policy'. Twelve years later Curtin would connect the two points by using wartime powers to transform Australia's economic framework—especially in respect of banking.

Curtin's policies were not only quite different from those of the Opposition, they were also much more radical than those of the Government. He could support the Government by attacking the Opposition, but he could not express enthusiasm for the cuts made by Acting PM Jim Fenton and Acting Treasurer Joe Lyons. 'There are conservative governments everywhere,' he said pointedly, and 'one of the most conservative is the present federal government'. Trapped by their political opponents, Curtin's colleagues were silent. His speech was the most substantial reply from the Government side; the succeeding Opposition speaker remarked that Curtin was 'the only honourable member opposite with sufficient courage to speak on the subject'. Reporter Warren Denning would write that 'Mr Curtin is probably the finest speaker the national parliament has produced since its transfer to Canberra [in 1927]'. He spoke entirely without passion or emotion, Denning recorded, but with great power.

Scullin returned from London in January 1931 and three weeks later reappointed Theodore Treasurer. In February Theodore pressed for an additional note issue to fund unemployment relief, as well as cuts to spending and wages. By early March, when Opposition Leader John Latham moved want of confidence in the Government's policies and the reappointment of Theodore as Treasurer, Labor had then been in office for seventeen difficult months. The economy had continued to deteriorate. Curtin spoke in the debate on 11 March 1931. He blamed the global monetary system and banks for falling wheat and wool prices. 'These problems affect not only Australia; they affect civilization itself', he said, and have their root 'in the entirely wrong policy which has marked post war monetary practice'. He blamed the gold standard, to which Chancellor of the Exchequer Winston Churchill had returned the United Kingdom in 1925, claiming that gold had increased in value while wheat had fallen in value (since the Australian pound was fixed against sterling, Australia had been returned to a gold standard as well). Curtin criticised the Senate's rejection of successive commodity marketing programs proposed by the Government. He supported Theodore's proposal for price stabilisation and 'the control of monetary policy by this Parliament'. The alternative plan proposed by NSW Premier Jack Lang was 'impractical'.

Curtin and Theodore were the most competent and best informed Labor spokesmen in the national economic debate. Both were deeply influenced by Keynes and they shared similar economic views. Though impressed with Theodore, however, Curtin was still close to Anstey. Curtin rated Anstey as 'the greatest figure in that Parliament', at least according to Denning, who for his part thought Anstey was the 'authentic genius' of the Scullin Cabinet. Curtin's friendship with Anstey may have cost him more than election to the first ministry in the Scullin government: according to Frank Green, it may also have prevented him winning a place when the ministry was reconstituted after Lyons and his allies left it. Green thought Anstey was 'probably the greatest orator and debater, with the exception of Alfred Deakin, that Parliament has known'.

But it was not so much Curtin's attachment to Anstey as their different roles in the Labor Caucus that drove him apart from Theodore. As a backbencher Curtin had more freedom to speak his mind. With a hostile Senate, a hostile Commonwealth Bank and difficult State premiers, as Commonwealth Treasurer Theodore was obliged to craft the best compromise he could. Like many of his Caucus colleagues Curtin could not bring himself to support the June Premiers' Plan under which State and Federal governments would reduce deficits in return for continued bank funding. As Treasurer, Theodore had little choice but to support it. Speaking in the House on 24 June 1931, Curtin explained that, 'My objection to the plan is that it seeks to isolate Australia's problems from the world situation. It entirely overlooks the fact that the difficulty is essentially a monetary one'. On the contrary, 'This plan abandons the Labour policy of monetary reform'.

With Theodore in the House, Curtin said the Premiers' Plan 'is in its essence the plan of the Party opposite' and that while it would require sacrifice from all Australians, it required none from overseas bond holders. Curtin argued that Labor should put its own plan, or permit its opponents to put their own plans. 'The Labor movement is faced, in connexion with this plan', he said, 'with what I recognize as a great crisis in its history and its structure'. Theodore interjected that 'the honourable member is becoming drunk with his own rhetoric'. Watching from the Press Gallery, Melbourne *Herald* reporter Angus McLachlan and his colleagues noted Theodore's slow delivery, intended to drive home the implied reference to Curtin's drinking problems. Ignoring it, Curtin responded that since Theodore challenged him, he would say he voted for his reinstatement in office 'because he fought the policy of deflation and the even more drastic economies which some were endeavoring to force upon the Labor Party'. He said, 'the personal or private transactions of any honourable member do not influence me in the least' and that 'I have never run away from anything in my life'. He concluded, 'I oppose this plan in its entirety'. Introduced by Scullin and argued by Theodore, the Premiers' Plan proposals were carried by the Opposition.

Curtin's core economic view remained that demand in a capitalist economy would not keep up with supply. He rejected Say's Law, the central tenet of classical economics, which affirms that supply creates its own demand. But his reasons for doing so had changed. In the Victorian Socialist Party days he thought competition between capitalists would hold wages too low for workers to buy the products they made. Wages had, however, increased. Curtin now blamed the banking system, claiming that the money supply or the growth of lending or credit were insufficient to finance the demand required to match increasing supply. The gold standard was part of the problem, because it restricted the amount of money in circulation to a multiple of the amount of gold held in the central bank. Curtin's changing emphasis no doubt reflected his reading of Keynes, who in his treatises on money sought monetary causes to explain recessions or deficient demand.

The Premiers' Plan was carried by the Opposition, but Labor was already hurtling toward a devastating defeat. At odds with their colleagues and deeply resentful of Theodore, Lyons and Fenton had resigned from Cabinet in early February 1931 and on 13 March they and three allies had crossed to the Opposition. Also in February, Lang's supporters in the Federal party split from the Scullin Government to form the six-member Federal Labor Party of New South Wales. When on 25 November 1931 they joined the Opposition in voting against the Government it lost its majority and, following the election, Lyons became Prime Minister leading the anti-Labor parties.

Despite the conflicts over policy, Curtin and Theodore had developed a mutual respect. Both lost their seats in

John Curtin, senior, with his two daughters and son John outside
Curtin's Golden Fleece Hotel at Charlton, Victoria, c. 1896.

Postcard with a portrait of the British socialist Tom Mann on the front, sent from Tom and Elsie Mann to John Curtin, 23 December 1910.

JCPML 00510/4 (RECORDS OF ROBIN GLENIE).

YOUR FRATERNAL COMRADE.
TOM MANN.

D.F.McK

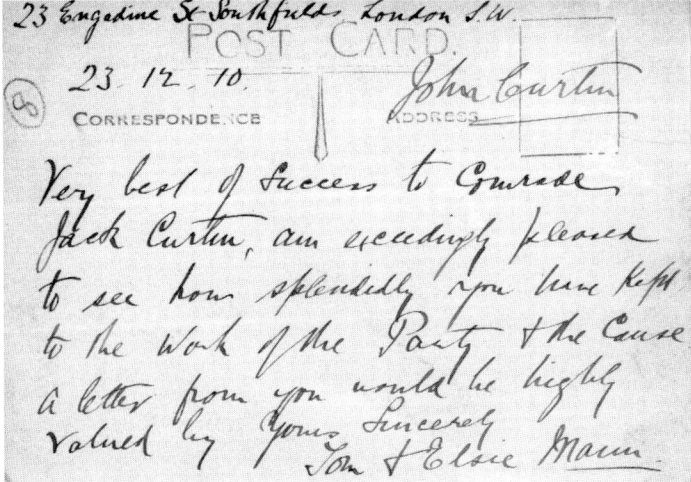

23 Engadine St Southfields London S.W.

POST CARD.

23. 12. 10.

John Curtin

CORRESPONDENCE

ADDRESS

Very best of success to Comrade Jack Curtin, am exceedingly pleased to see how splendidly you have kept to the Work of the Party & the Cause a letter from you would be highly valued by

Yours sincerely
Tom & Elsie Mann

The sort of thing that induces tarts to go in for mixed bathing.

John Curtin at
the beach and the
message on the
reverse (above) (n.d.).
JCPML 00225/2 (RECORDS
OF PETER CURTIN).

John Curtin with Frank Anstey, his political ally, during the Depression (n.d.). JCPML 00409/4 (RECORDS OF WEST AUSTRALIAN NEWS LTD). COURTESY OF WEST AUSTRALIAN NEWS LTD.

John Curtin relaxing with his friend and driver, Ray Tracey, c. 1944. JCPML 00412/11: RECORDS OF THE *HERALD & WEEKLY TIMES*. COURTESY OF THE *HERALD & WEEKLY TIMES*.

Elsie and John Curtin in the grounds of the Prime Minister's Lodge, Canberra, 1942. JCPML 00004/28 (RECORDS OF THE CURTIN FAMILY).

General Jan Smuts (South Africa), William Lyon Mackenzie King (Canada), Winston Churchill (United Kingdom), John Curtin (Australia) and Peter Fraser (New Zealand) at the Dominion Prime Ministers' Conference, London, 1944. JCPML 00004/31 (RECORDS OF THE CURTIN FAMILY).

Former journalist John Curtin meets the Canberra Press Gallery, known as 'The Circus', c. 1945. JCPML 00376/2 (RECORDS OF THE CURTIN FAMILY).

News of John Curtin's death is displayed at a Salvation Army stall on Vasey Highway, Balikpapan, Borneo, 5 July 1945. JCPML 00409/21 (RECORDS OF WEST AUSTRALIAN NEWS LTD). COURTESY OF WEST AUSTRALIAN NEWS LTD.

Robert Gordon Menzies at John Curtin's funeral, 1945. JCPML 00347/70 (RECORDS OF WEST AUSTRALIAN NEWS LTD). COURTESY OF WEST AUSTRALIAN NEWS LTD.

Gun-carriage bearing John Curtin's coffin outside the funeral home, 1945. JCPML 00347/23 (RECORDS OF WEST AUSTRALIAN NEWS LTD). COURTESY OF WEST AUSTRALIAN NEWS LTD.

A crowd of over 20,000 people attending John Curtin's funeral at Karrakatta, Western Australia, 1945. JCPML 00041/1 (RECORDS OF MARGARET STILES).

the electoral rout that terminated the Scullin Government in 1931. Theodore never returned to Federal politics, and instead entered a profitable business partnership with media baron Frank Packer. He encouraged Curtin to hope for the leadership of the Labor Party, if he could control his drinking. 'Dear Jack', he wrote after Curtin's defeat in Fremantle, 'Your defeat is a sad personal misfortune, for you could have done good work in Opposition and established your claims to ultimate leadership of the Federal forces. I have long believed you are destined for great things, if you could keep hold of yourself, and if that old hag, fate, is not too relentless'. For his part Curtin wrote to him in September 1932 urging him to come back as Leader. In an answering letter the following month Theodore wrote he had not lost faith in his policies, 'but my faith in the intelligence of the workers is sadly shaken'. Curtin's friendship with Anstey had divided them. Now Anstey, too, was leaving politics and would not re-contest his seat in 1934. Theodore could not help waspishly noting that he had heard Anstey was now living in Sydney and 'making his obeisances to the Langites'. Curtin's friendship with Anstey had evidently cooled, perhaps because Anstey was drifting toward Lang. As Prime Minister Curtin appointed Theodore in February 1942 to establish and direct an Allied Works Council. As Opposition Leader he later refused Anstey's request for nomination to the royal commission into the banking system.

Back home in Perth Curtin for a time made his living partly by writing about horse racing. At the nomination of the state Labor Government he became chairman of a three-man commission to prepare Western Australia's case to the Commonwealth Grants Commission. Familiarity with Commonwealth–State financial relations brought him to a recognition of the problems involved, and the conviction that some solution should be found. Though he would within a few years make the greatest change to the relationship between the Commonwealth and the States in the history of the Federation, in the 1930s he did not believe there was a great issue of principle involved. It was, he said, an issue of administrative effectiveness.

Returned to Federal Parliament as member for Fremantle in the general election on 15 September 1934, when Scullin resigned the leadership in October the following year Curtin was elected Leader of the Opposition in a close ballot. Curtin won on his evident ability, and his refusal during the Depression either to desert the Party or to accept the policies that as a Government it believed itself obliged to put forward. He would be Opposition Leader for six years, and his highest priority was to unite a divided and depleted party to prepare it for a return to government. He continued to be interested in economic policy, however, and to dwell on the lessons of the Depression. Responding to the July 1937 *Report of the Royal Commission on the Australian Monetary and Banking System* (the Napier Commission), for example, Curtin blamed the Bruce–Page Government for giving independence to the Board of the Commonwealth Bank in 1924, and thus giving away the Government's right to determine policy. The Royal Commission had recommended that when required the policy of the Federal Government must be given effect by the Board of the Commonwealth Bank, a provision which in modified form is the law today. Curtin wrote that a Labor Government would make that a 'positive fact'. He wrote that 'National control of the means of exchange is a fundamental principle of the Labor Movement', and required 'national control of the banking system' and 'national control of banking policy and of the instruments of exchange'. The future Labor Treasurer Ben Chifley was a member of the Napier Commission. Significantly, Curtin did not endorse Chifley's minority recommendation for the nationalisation of all banking.

Curtin was certainly not opposed to tariff protection for Australian manufacturing industry, but he was more moderate in his support than many of his colleagues. 'It was not for nothing, nor idly', Denning wrote, 'did Mr Curtin announce just before Easter of 1936 that in its future tariff policy, the Labor Party intended to apply the principles of "new protection"; that is, protection to be granted only to those industries which in turn freely grant their employees decent wages and working conditions'. Reporting the 'extravaganza' of the Scullin Government's tariff increases from late 1929, Denning said that Western Australian members murmured against high protection or rather 'excessive and unintelligent protection'. The Western Australian source would almost certainly have been Curtin, with whom Denning was very close.

With the outbreak of war with Germany in 1939 Curtin's thoughts turned to the wartime economy, financing the war effort and sharing the burden. In speech after speech he demonstrated easy familiarity with concepts and numbers. In a speech on the Budget Menzies brought down within a week of the declaration of war Curtin pointed out that over the past three years revenue had increased much more than defence spending. The increase in revenue had come from indirect taxes such as tariffs. Through income tax concessions the Government had redirected the tax burden away from income tax on the well-to-do and more to indirect tax on the consumer. He wanted higher taxes on the rich, and less borrowing. The Commonwealth should not continue to 'borrow from the rich to enable us to finance the war, whilst continuing to tax the poor'. He recalled that while orthodox theory held that development could not proceed faster than the resources the central bank was prepared to provide, 'all the banking and financial theories which had been adhered to throughout the world prior to 4th of August 1914, as the only principles upon which banking and finance could be satisfactorily conducted, were thrown overboard immediately after the war commenced'. So, too, Japan had financed the development of its secondary industries as had Germany, and 'whence came the money?'. The war might be ended by shortage of shells or by shortage of men, but never by shortage of money. The truth is that 'responsibility for financial policy in this country doesn't lie with the trading banks. It does not even lie with the Commonwealth Bank.

It lies with this Parliament and with the Government which is responsible to this Parliament . . . Responsibility for financial and monetary policy is here'. In January 1941 noting that Menzies' Budget had assumed central bank loans, Curtin said the Commonwealth Bank 'did for our opponents on the outbreak of war' what it had refused to do for Labor in 1930—extend central bank credit.

7

Prime Minister Curtin
Changes Australia

When Prime Minister Artie Fadden lost the support of the two independents who held the balance of power in the House of Representatives early in October 1941, Curtin was asked to form Government. Once in office and despite not having a majority in either the House of Representatives or in the Senate, Curtin moved swiftly to implement his program. It was designed to meet the challenges of war, but much of it addressed the problems of economic management that had become apparent in the Depression. Even before Japan entered the war Curtin was energetically reshaping Australia; after Pearl Harbor the changes became more profound.

The new Cabinet first convened in Parliament House at 12.15 p.m. on Tuesday 7 October 1941, the day Curtin became Prime Minister and the Cabinet members were sworn in by the Governor General. It was necessary to prepare a Budget 'without any delay', the new Prime Minister told his Cabinet. Three weeks after he became Prime Minister the new Government introduced the Budget. In a radio address that evening Curtin said it had not been possible to go through every item in three weeks of office, but the Budget would increase soldiers' pay and old age pensions, and it would shift the tax burden. He also announced a legislative change he had sought for decades. 'The Government intends to give effect immediately to certain recommendations of the Royal Commission on the Monetary and Banking Systems to bring the operations of the trading banks under effective control.' The Budget 'proposes to draw upon central bank credit to finance expansion of production' and 'establishes proper control of the trading banks through the Commonwealth Bank acting under a policy laid down by the Treasurer on behalf of the Government'. He had thus within weeks of taking office seized for the Commonwealth the authority that had been denied it during the Depression, and which it would ever after hold.

Scullin had at least had a majority in the House, so on the face of it Curtin's hold on power was more fragile than his Labor predecessor's a decade before. It would not be until after the general election of August 1943, a battle carefully prepared by Curtin to entrench an enduring Labor majority, that he could command the House of Representatives let alone the Senate. But war with Germany and Italy strengthened Curtin's power, and the Japanese attack on Pearl Harbor eight weeks after he was appointed Prime Minister consolidated his position. Able to invoke the Constitutional defence power freely and facing a compliant, shocked Opposition, Curtin had more power than any other Australian prime minister in history. He used the threat to drive changes that would otherwise be blocked by a hostile Senate, by the States, or by his dependence on the votes of independents in the House. If there were no other way, the defence power in the Constitution offered wide authority to a federal government in wartime. 'A transformation as great as that which this government regards as imperative is inevitably beset with many difficulties and must create many problems,' Curtin said following the outbreak of war with Japan. The war footing would nonetheless require 'the reshaping, in fact, the revolutionizing, of the Australian way of life quickly, efficiently and without question'. Required by the circumstances of war, many of the changes were ones proposed by Labor and rejected by its opponents during the Depression, and most would become permanent parts of the Australian framework.

By 10 February Curtin was able to announce a National Economic Plan that included pegging wages and profits, closing down non-essential industries and directing manpower, and which represented the first stage of movement to a total war economy. Nine days later Chifley announced more details, including Cabinet's decision to exclude the States from income tax. From uniform taxation and central banking the Curtin Government moved quickly in 1942 to problems of postwar planning. By May Curtin told Parliament the Government was giving consideration to postwar arrangements for social security. In the same statement he said the Tariff Board had been given authority to make reports on the economic adjustments that might be expected after the war when, he said in August 1942, 'there will have to be a fairer distribution of wealth'. He made a promise of postwar full employment the centrepiece of his 1943 election campaign, and initiated the writing of a white paper on full employment on his return from London in June 1944.

While pressing for a full employment policy in Australia, the Curtin Government also participated in negotiations that led to the creation of the International Monetary Fund and the World Bank and later to the creation of global trading rules in the General Agreement on Tariffs and Trade (GATT). Uniform taxation, modern central banking, the full employment policy and Australia's engagement with the world through the IMF, the World Bank and GATT— all pillars of Australia's postwar economy—thus emerged from the Curtin Government.

So, too, Curtin oversaw the beginning of the postwar immigration program, the beginning of Commonwealth support for university education, the beginning of the Commonwealth's housing program, and big changes to social security—all of which would remain important Federal policies in the decades to come.

Curtin has almost disappeared from this story of the transformation of the Australian economy, in favour of his successor and Treasurer Ben Chifley. There is no doubt Chifley had a major role in economic matters and would normally have brought Treasury matters to Cabinet. It was also a very busy and urgent period, so ministers had a great deal of autonomy within their areas. Curtin necessarily relied on Chifley as Treasurer and on the other senior Cabinet ministers. After Japan entered the war Cabinet endorsed a split in responsibilities, with a War Cabinet presided over by Curtin and a Production Executive Committee, to deal with some economic and financial matters, presided over by the Treasurer. Responsibility for the huge works program required by the fighting services was given to what became the Allied Works Council, run by Theodore.

The evidence suggests that Curtin was closely involved in all major decisions while he was Prime Minister, and certainly on all major economic policy decisions. In conversation with reporter Harold Cox, Curtin criticised Churchill for failing to involve himself in the economic direction of the war, a criticism Curtin would not have made if he had done the same. Major economic issues such as government spending and taxes, finance, trade and international economic relationships were dealt with by the Full Cabinet, which Curtin chaired. Economic and financial issues were also important issues in the Advisory War Council, which Curtin chaired and of which Chifley was not a member. Though he had a multitude of responsibilities Curtin had two economic advisers, Douglas Copland

and Richard Downing, who were involved in the development of major policies across the government. Curtin as well as Chifley often attended meetings with the chairman and the governor of the Commonwealth Bank, which dealt with financial issues.

Chifley himself freely acknowledged Curtin's authority. Outlining the Budget proposals for the coming year to Full Cabinet on 7 July 1942, for example, Chifley said that 'a certain figure had been fixed on as an estimate of war expenditure'. He personally had set the figure higher, 'but after consultation with the Prime Minister the lower figure had been adopted'. One reason Curtin had strong views on the level of spending in that instance was that he had strong views on the level of taxation. At the same Full Cabinet meeting Curtin referred to an announcement he had made that tax would not be increased in the coming year, a principle then endorsed by the Cabinet meeting.

Chifley controlled the financial affairs of the government but the record shows that Curtin took an interest in economic issues before Chifley, that he read, spoke and wrote about them more deeply, that he took a more prominent role in party and public debates on economic issues through his political career, and that he came to Government in October 1941 with strong views based on his reading, his experiences of the Scullin Government and the Depression and on his understanding of Australian economic institutions, and that he proceeded to methodically execute these ideas into policy. Curtin had been around long enough to become jaded with economic ideas. 'I have attended the funeral of so many economic theories', he told economist L.F. Giblin.

As early as May 1940, nineteen months before Japan entered the war, Curtin as Leader of the Opposition had moved in Caucus for a special conference of the party to determine the principles of postwar reconstruction. Not only did he come to office with a program, but within a year he was also working on an explicit postwar agenda, one which envisaged full employment at home and membership of new global economic institutions that would allow Australia to participate in the direction of the world economy. Those initiatives were also ascribed to Chifley, though Curtin had at least an equal claim as the initiator and moving spirit. It is obscured in the record, but it was clear enough to contemporaries. 'Curtin I would rate very high, above Chifley', economist Leslie Melville, who worked with them both, remarked in his oral history. 'I think he was an abler man. Curtin, when he took over during the war, made his decisions very quickly.' Interviewed not long before he died, Melville recalled that Chifley's skill was in financial affairs, but Curtin had a better grasp of economic issues and a deeper interest.

The immediate transformation of the Commonwealth Bank into a true central bank with authority over trading banks, and the equally rapid monopolisation of income taxing power by the Commonwealth are two important examples of Curtin's determination to effect in wartime what would be extremely difficult to carry out in peace.

Two others are Australia's role in Allied negotiations on global economic arrangements, and the adoption of a full employment policy for Australia. These four central policies became the pillars of modern Commonwealth government.

Ten days after the new government was sworn in Treasurer Ben Chifley told Cabinet that a conference had been arranged for Monday 20 October between Curtin and Chifley, and the Commonwealth Bank. The major issue Curtin and Chifley wished to discuss with the Bank was precisely the issue on which Sir Robert Gibson had refused any direction or advice almost exactly twelve years before. There was, Chifley told Cabinet on 18 October, a £100 million gap between expected Commonwealth revenue and expected spending, not all of which could be covered by new loans from the public.

At that October 1929 meeting Scullin had apologised to the Governor for uncivil remarks by Frank Anstey. With Australia at war and Curtin and Chifley unhesitatingly wielding the defence power, the atmosphere at the 20 October meeting was evidently quite different. Meeting with the Chairman of the Commonwealth Bank Board, Sir Claude Reading, and the Governor of the Bank, Hugh Armitage, Curtin and Chifley discussed not only the bridging of the gap in the Budget, but also the Government direction of monetary policy, control of private banks, rates of interest and extension of the activities of the Commonwealth Bank.

The Commonwealth Bank and the trading banks were indignant but helpless. Briefing trading bank representatives in Sydney a week after the meeting with the new Government, Sir Claude reported that the Prime Minister and Treasurer were quite determined. 'The Government intends control of the banking system', he told the five trading bank executives, and while he and Armitage had discussed it very fully with Curtin and Chifley they had not succeeded 'in having the Government's policy changed in any major respect'. The position of the Commonwealth Bank would be affected as well as that of the trading banks, Sir Claude said. The independent authority of the Commonwealth Bank would be lessened. One banker asked if it were quite definite that control of the banking system was to be taken away from the present authorities and vested in the Treasurer. Sir Claude said this was so, but that it would be done by regulation that would automatically lapse after the war. It seemed the only possibility of this not happening would be if the Senate were to disallow the regulation. Sir Claude told the banks he did not think the Commonwealth Bank could do anything more to fight the case for the trading banks and if it did so it would lose its own influence with the Government. The bankers considered the possibility of fighting. One banker asked if the trading banks and perhaps the Commonwealth Bank should warn the public of the dangers in the Government's policy. Reading and Armitage thought not at this stage, but 'an issue on the volume of central bank credit to be released might arise between the Government and the Commonwealth Bank at a later stage'.

In his 29 October 1941 national broadcast marking the new Government's first budget Curtin announced that his Government 'proposes to draw upon central bank credit to finance expansion of production' and establish 'proper control of the trading banks through the Commonwealth Bank acting under a policy laid down by the Treasurer on behalf of the Government'. While the Commonwealth Bank would be brought under control of the Treasurer, its powers over the trading banks would be increased. The Commonwealth Bank would have regulatory authority to instruct the trading banks, and the Government authority to instruct the Commonwealth Bank. It was, as Noel Butlin wrote in his official history of the war economy, 'a revolutionary change in the position of the Commonwealth Bank as a central bank'. The previous Government had sought to increase the powers of the Commonwealth Bank by the consent of the trading banks; the Curtin Government entrenched it in regulations invoking the overriding defence power of the Common-wealth Constitution. The National Security (Banking) Regulations were issued on 26 November 1941, two weeks before Japan attacked. 'Consideration for the postwar position no doubt had a part in the Government's decision' to use the defence powers rather than voluntary cooper-ation, economist L.F. Giblin shrewdly observed. 'The wisdom of its decision in this matter became fully evident, even to itself, only when the war ended.' What was secured with the defence power when Labor lacked a majority in either house would later be secured by legislation when, after the 1943 election, it commanded a majority in both.

Chifley had day-to-day responsibility but Curtin remained much more closely involved in the development of the banking and monetary policy than contemporary Australian prime ministers. He attended many meetings with the chairman and the governor of the Commonwealth Bank, usually with Chifley though occasionally without him. On 8 December, the same day Curtin chaired Full Cabinet and War Cabinet discussions on Japan's entry to the war, he joined Chifley and Treasury Secretary Stuart McFarlane to meet with Reading, Armitage and Commonwealth Bank economist Leslie Melville in Melbourne. At issue was the growing gap between the spending required for the war, and the amount that could be raised by taxation and loans. Reading thought the gap would now be around £55 million, taking the form of unredeemed Treasury bills at the end of June 1942. He urged the Government to increase revenue from taxes or to increase the total amount of savings that might fund new war loans. Rationing would also be necessary. Armitage added that government war spending financed by the banking system was placing large amounts of money in the hands of the people and that unless this was taken from them in some way there was a serious danger of excessive purchasing power leading to inflation. According to the Bank record, Curtin did not seem inclined to commit himself 'beyond general acceptance of the proposition that spending power would need to be curtailed'.

Through 1942 the Commonwealth Bank was concerned by the increasing gap between spending, and the total of loans and taxation. The difference was made up by treasury bills, which were essentially central bank credit creation. It was therefore with considerable alarm that Reading and Armitage read in the *Sydney Morning Herald* on 12 June 1942 Curtin's statement that the Government had decided there would be no increase in tax rates for companies or individuals in the 1942–43 Budget. They requested a meeting with Curtin and Chifley, which took place on 3 July. Armitage's notes of the meeting are some of the best of the few detailed records we have of Curtin's behind-the-scenes work on economic policy. The Curtin they reveal is a politician completely on top of the issues, candid and tough minded, with a strong strategic sense, determined to override the concerns of the chairman and governor of the Bank in pursuit of his wider aim of effecting a permanent transformation of Australian institutions. It is also perfectly plain, as from the entire Reserve Bank of Australia (RBA) archive, that Reading and Armitage and for that matter Chifley regarded Curtin as the ultimate source of authority in economic affairs.

By then the expected war spending had increased to £450 million and the gap after taxes, Lease/Lend credits and war loans had increased to £150 million. Curtin told the meeting he doubted the whole £450 million could be spent 'as practically all manpower and womanpower necessary had already been diverted into war channels'. Reading pressed for 'further direct taxation on the lower income groups which constituted the largest part of the Australian national income'. Curtin was quite clear in his response.

> The Prime Minister replied that with the fate of uniform taxation in the balance he was not even prepared to think of increasing direct taxation for the present. He pointed out that one of the strongest objections to uniform taxation was the possibility of the Commonwealth putting rates up and to overcome this he had given an assurance to both the public and to the States that no increase in direct taxation would be made in 1941–42 income which would be taxed during 1942–43. Furthermore, he had in mind that it might be necessary to hold a referendum on the question of uniform taxation and it would be fatal to such a referendum if the public held the opinion that rates were likely to be increased. After considerable discussion he went so far as to say that when the fate of uniform taxation had been definitely decided, he might be prepared to consider further direct taxation.

Curtin had not only imposed Commonwealth government control on the central bank and central bank control on the private banks; he was now using the new authority over credit to ease the transition to Commonwealth control over income tax. The two were closely related, because with a fully empowered central bank under its direction and with growing control over the bulk of Australian government spending, revenues and borrowing, the Commonwealth would for the first time in its history have the means to control the booms and busts of the Australian economy.

In the four decades of Australian Federation before Curtin became Prime Minister, the governments of the major States were more important than the Federal Government. They were after all the successors to the colonial governments, and they designed the Federal constitution to ensure they remained powerful, independent and well funded. Curtin made the Commonwealth pre-eminent, and it would remain so. He changed the nature of the Australian Federation forever. He did it by cutting off State government access to income tax and limiting State government access to loans, at the same time as he took the Commonwealth into new areas of activity.

Pressed by the vast spending increases required to fund the mobilisation of Australia against Japan, the new Government needed more loans from the public, and higher tax revenues. As we have seen, Curtin was not by conviction a centralist. He came from a small and remote State that had always insisted on its rights within the Federation. But he did think Federal–State relations should be arranged by administrative convenience. It was, he thought, now very inconvenient indeed that the States should be able to impose income taxes when the responsibilities of the Commonwealth were so great. It would be very much better if the Commonwealth imposed a single scale of income tax nationally, and handed back to the States what they needed. As to determining what the States needed, that would chiefly be the decision of the Commonwealth.

It was also impossible to allow the States to continue to borrow to fund their own projects, when the Commonwealth needed to command the resources to build airfields, ports, barracks and roads to meet the Japanese threat. Meeting on 15 December, a week after Pearl Harbor, Curtin told a meeting of Full Cabinet in Canberra that 'it would be necessary for the Commonwealth to take over the loan commitments of the Loan Council as a Commonwealth liability'. Instead of States borrowing for their own purposes, 'the Commonwealth would make advances to the States and keep in the closest touch with the States as to how the money would be spent'. It would be another half century before the States regained the right to borrow on their own authority.

Curtin had announced his National Economic Plan on 10 February 1942. On the 19th Chifley announced more details, including Cabinet's decision to exclude the States from income tax. Two days before Chifley's announcement, a Full Cabinet meeting in Sydney had authorised a complete mobilisation of Australian resources in the war effort, with ministers believing that 'the Commonwealth's authority, whether or not it impinged on the wishes of the States as regards the use of manpower, material etc should be supreme'.

At a 22 April Premiers' Conference Curtin asked the Premiers to agree to uniform Commonwealth income tax for the duration of the war and one year afterward. Curtin told the Premiers that in the development of Australia 'there has been no complete sovereignty in the Commonwealth Parliament' but now, whatever one's views, whatever the past history, there exists 'the overwhelming necessity of immediately organizing the nation for the most terrible and crucial ordeal the nation has ever faced'. He added that 'Neither the sovereignty of the States, nor unification, nor any other political philosophy in this country, is attainable unless the war is won', and winning the war required a uniform Commonwealth taxation. The Premiers refused, Curtin explaining that some States 'have said that, however sincere might be the Commonwealth to terminate this arrangement a year after the war, its commitments would be so great as to induce it to hold on to the taxable resources. I do not think that will be the case'. Those sceptical Premiers proved to be right.

A few weeks later, on 5 May, Chifley announced that the Government was having Bills prepared for the Parliament and that it had no doubt it had constitutional authority to impose uniform taxation. By early June Curtin had guided the Bills through both the House and a hostile Senate, against the furious opposition of the States. His State Labor colleagues were as hostile as the non-Labor Premiers. NSW Labor Premier Bill McKell unsuccessfully challenged uniform income tax at the NSW ALP Conference in 1942, and Labor Premiers in Queensland and Western Australia later joined an unsuccessful challenge to the legislation in the High Court. It was a striking testament to Curtin's political skills that the legislation was passed by both Federal chambers. It required, as he told the Commonwealth Bank, a public commitment by Curtin not to raise taxes at a time when they should certainly have been raised. As a result of his daring, the single biggest enhancement of the Commonwealth's powers since Federation in 1901 had become law.

Henceforth the Commonwealth would make general or 'untied' grants to the States, compensating them for the loss of income tax. Established in 1933 to assess State requests for special grants, the Commonwealth Grants Commission was after 1942 responsible for recommending on the distribution of the very much larger annual grants from Commonwealth income tax revenue. On the principle of fiscal equalisation it tilted the mix so States with a smaller tax base and bigger needs received back in grants more per head than the wealthier states. Because the amounts of revenue were now so much greater, this principle of horizontal fiscal equalisation would become a major principle of Australian federalism. But the Commonwealth's role would not end at making untied grants to the States. Increasingly the Commonwealth would also offer conditional grants, which required that the money be spent on specific programs in education, health, housing and other areas in which the Commonwealth might have a concurrent constitutional power with the States, or no power at all other than the power to make grants for specific purposes.

The Commonwealth could now more profoundly influence the States through its control over the major source of revenue. It could also fund a direct expansion of activity in the areas in which it either had or could acquire specific constitutional authority.

Curtin believed Tom Mann's injunction that education was the key. In 1943 Minister for War Organisation of Industry John Dedman announced in the House that the Federal Government would support university students enrolled in reserve courses, not only to support the war effort but also because the peace would require 'the devoted application of the best brains this country possesses'. He acknowledged his plan would have 'profound social implications' because 'once we have introduced the principle that university education in any courses shall be open to the ablest students, however small their financial resources, we have taken a long step forward. Personally, I hope Australia will never go back on that principle'. From that long step forward came the postwar Commonwealth Reconstruction Training Scheme for ex-servicemen's education, the Australian National University and then the Federal commitment to fund university education. The postwar Menzies Government is generally credited with developing Commonwealth support for higher education, which it certainly did. But the Commonwealth role began under Curtin.

The postwar immigration program that transformed Australia's population also began under Curtin. The Full Cabinet had appointed an inter-departmental committee on migration as early as October 1943, and by May 1944 had laid down a detailed policy, including assisted passage for (white) British people. With some hesitation it was broadened to include Maltese—so long as they had a working knowledge of English. Before the war Maltese had been excluded as insufficiently white. By the end of 1944 the Curtin Government was committed to the resumption of large-scale immigration from the UK and northwestern Europe, but also (if necessary) from southern and eastern Europe.

Commonwealth control over income tax paid for the immigration program, which Curtin's Government adopted as a postwar policy objective. It funded development projects such as the Snowy River Scheme, first mooted under the Chifley Government. It allowed the Commonwealth to expand its role in tertiary education. But the biggest change at the time was the expansion of the Commonwealth role in social security. Over time the States would stop offering old age pension and unemployment relief, and the Commonwealth would take over. Curtin introduced widows' pensions in 1942, and in February the following year Chifley announced the beginnings of a 'National Welfare Scheme'. In the first instance it provided funeral benefits for pensioners and a new form of maternity allowance, and by 1945 included unemployment and sickness benefits. In 1944 and 1945 legislation was passed to allow hospital and pharmaceutical benefits. Though the 'fourteen powers' referendum to widely extend Commonwealth authority was defeated in 1944 (Curtin was lukewarm in support, and campaigned without vigour), the Commonwealth acquired clear and wide powers over social services in a 1946 referendum. None of these extensions of Commonwealth activity could have occurred without Commonwealth control over income tax.

By controlling tax revenue the Commonwealth was over time able to increase its own spending, and gain greater control over spending by the States. Keynes had suggested that governments could smooth out economic fluctuations by taxing more than they spent during upswings, and spending more than they taxed during downswings. Curtin had acquired for the Commonwealth the necessary economic weight to implement the theory.

Curtin effected the biggest shift to Commonwealth authority since Federation, but he was not a passionate centralist. Unlike Evatt, who pressed for the widest possible constitutional powers for the Commonwealth, Curtin was very clearly focused only on those additional powers he believed necessary to carry out the Commonwealth's economic responsibilities. When the issue of a proposed referendum on Commonwealth powers came up at Cabinet in October 1943, he told his colleagues that 'the Commonwealth should not ask for more than was necessary to carry out its obligations', and there was 'no need to aim at unification. The States had certain necessary functions and they should retain powers appropriate to their obligations and status'. He told Cabinet the following month he thought three powers were absolutely necessary to enable the Government to do its national duty: banking, employment and power over trade and commerce. The Commonwealth already had banking, and the agreement he had made with the States included in substance the remaining powers. Powers over housing and education were useful, but they were not indispensable.

As Prime Minister, after achieving control of both houses, after more than four decades of political experience, Curtin still thought Commonwealth power over banking was the most important of those additional powers that were absolutely necessary to enable the government to do its duty. He was still the child of the financial panic of the 1890s. To a very large extent the history of the first half-century of the Federal Labor Parliamentary Party, from the Banking Bill of 1911 to the conflict between Scullin, Theodore and Gibson, to the immediate declaration by Curtin and Chifley of Commonwealth authority over banking when they came to office in 1941 and, finally, to the disastrous postwar decision of Ben Chifley to nationalise the banks, was one of asserting Commonwealth control over money and credit. So it would remain. In the early 1970s Prime Minister Gough Whitlam would extend Commonwealth regulatory authority to include all financial institutions. The next Labor Prime Minister, Bob Hawke, and his treasurer Paul Keating, would float the currency and remove many controls from banking. One effect was to increase the authority of the Reserve Bank of Australia, because it was no longer required to use its powers to achieve an exchange rate objective set by Treasury. Though the postwar Menzies Government amended Chifley's central banking legislation to reintroduce a board, the Commonwealth's last-resort power to direct the Bank was retained in the legislation and remains today. The Commonwealth Treasurer has conferred on the Bank an independent authority to make monetary policy, but it is a conditional independence to pursue a policy of low inflation, sustainable output and employment growth. Were the circumstances ever grave enough to require it, the Commonwealth has the legal authority to regain direct control over monetary policy.

Curtin was a child during the depression of the 1890s and as an adult witnessed both the slump that followed World War I and the Great Depression. Because of those experiences his highest economic priority was that everyone capable of working should be able to work. The commitment was all the more pressing because it was widely assumed massive unemployment could well follow the end of World War II, just as it had followed the end of World War I. His Government's commitment to full employment found its most memorable expression in a white paper issued in the last months of Curtin's life, but he was committed to full employment from the beginning of his Government. On 29 April 1942, for example, Curtin told Parliament that 'as early as practicable an effort should be made to make certain that an opportunity will be given to every man and woman to obtain employment'. In Full Cabinet on 9 June 1942, a time when the Japanese threat was still pressing, Curtin said he wanted 'adequate machinery' in place to deal with demobilisation, even if it meant the Government risked a premature approach to the problem. In his Budget speech of 2 September 1942 Chifley also mentioned a commitment to full employment. And on 24 November 1942 in a speech to the Constitutional Convention, Curtin announced that the Government's postwar objective would be full employment. Of the three goals of employment, improved living standards and national development, he said it was 'only natural to place the greatest emphasis on employment' given the still fresh memories of the Depression. In his policy speech of 26 July 1943 Curtin stated that the Government 'pledges itself to ensure that every man and woman of the forces who, on discharge is in need of employment, will be provided with reasonable opportunities for such employment'.

The origins of the famous White Paper that expressed the Australian Government's commitment to postwar full employment are now obscure. But it was Curtin who made a promise of postwar full employment a centrepiece of his 1943 election campaign, and it was Curtin who on his return in June 1944 from his visit to the United Kingdom and North America instructed the preparation of a white paper on full employment, on the model of the white paper recently published in the UK. He issued a press statement on 7 July 1944 commending the British White Paper, which he had tabled in the House on 21 July. At the time he announced that 'I shall be able shortly to lay before this Parliament a document broadly comparable in scope with the British White Paper'. Curtin assigned the task to H.C. ('Nugget') Coombs as Director-General of the Ministry of Post-War Reconstruction.

With a quite small permanent bureaucracy including only a few well-trained economists, much of the economic advisory work during the war (as during the Depression) was handed out to formal or informal groups of academic and other outside economists and public servants whose actual work and responsibilities often did not correspond to their titles. The most important of these groups was the Financial and Economic Advisory Committee (always referred to as 'F&E') set up under Menzies in 1939 and chaired by Melbourne University economics professor L.F. Giblin. (The informality of the actual arrangements is suggested by Melville, who said that 'if there was a chairman, it was Giblin'.) Its members included Douglas Copland, who was economic adviser to Prime Minister Menzies and then Prime Minister Curtin, and Coombs. It performed a variety of tasks, including reviewing the negotiations for the IMF, World Bank and GATT, and reviewing some of the drafts of the white paper on full employment.

After many early drafts the full employment paper was first submitted to Cabinet for further discussion on 20 March 1945 and tabled on 30 May. Curtin wrote extensive comments on a draft, probably between 15 March and 20 March. In his comments written on a copy of the draft proposed by Coombs, Curtin objected to the creation of a Central Planning Office and a National Investment

Board, two phrases that suggested an intention to override the views of State governments, to a specific numerical target for unemployment and to increasing the share of national income going to wages. All these changes demonstrated a somewhat more cautious approach than the drafters, and all of Curtin's changes would be approved by mainstream economists today. He also deleted a passage that opposed exchange rate changes to help the balance of payments, and which referred to expected IMF rules that would impose strict conditions on any changes in the rate. Coombs recalled that:

> There was no significant difference between Curtin and Chifley. They worked together all the way through and I think if there had been any differences, Chifley would have given way . . . Curtin relied very much on Chifley's economic and financial knowledge and was guided by him, but there was no uncertainty as to where the final yes or no lay and that was with Curtin.

From the early 1930s Curtin's economic thought mostly centred on how the existing system could be better run. What he had to say about money, credit and government deficits was very close to what Keynes thought, and Curtin's informal evolution to these views was paralleled by a similar change among academically trained economists. By the beginning of World War II, when many of them would take on new roles as members of F&E and advisers in Canberra, Australian economists were mostly Keynesian. As Dick Downing, Curtin's wartime assistant economic adviser recalled, 'by the time I got back from Cambridge in mid-1939 we were all Keynesians'. The Commonwealth Bank's economist in the 1930s, Leslie Melville, concurred: the Keynesian revolution was much quicker in Australia than either the United States or the United Kingdom. As an admirer of Keynes' earlier work, with long held under-consumptionist views and now surrounded by economists influenced by Keynes, it is highly likely that as Prime Minister Curtin thought in an essentially Keynesian framework.

Many wartime plans did not survive the end of the conflict but, as Butlin and Schedvin argued, 'what was to survive was the abiding commitment to full employment'. In the narrow sense full employment meant that every adult who wanted a job could get a job, but in a wider sense it meant that available labour and capital would be fully utilised and that government would use its powers over taxes, spending and the financial system to smooth out economic fluctuations. For the next quarter century Australia enjoyed rapid growth and low unemployment. Under the impact of oil price increases and rapid wage increases in the 1970s the commitment to full employment collided with a commitment to low and steady inflation. It would be the end of the twentieth century before low, steady inflation and sustained full employment existed simultaneously, and even then the level of unemployment was much greater than the full employment envisaged in 1945.

The goal of full employment was not always attained, but the Commonwealth now had the powers to stabilise the booms and busts of Curtin's lifetime. The central bank had control over interest rates, the exchange rate and the lending of commercial banks and, directly or indirectly, the Commonwealth could influence the central bank. The Commonwealth now had control over borrowing by Australian governments, and over the major share of government revenue and government spending. Because of the powers seized for the Commonwealth in the first eight months of the Curtin Government, it could not only vastly extend the sphere of Commonwealth activity, but also plausibly commit itself to the maintenance of full employment. More than half a century later those powers were still the most important economic tools possessed by the Commonwealth, and were being used to attain the same goals. Defining the goal of full employment and acquiring the tools to achieve it, Curtin created Australia's Keynesian revolution. The socialist who believed that capitalism would always produce too much and consume too little became the Prime Minister who acquired for the Commonwealth the means to balance supply and demand in a successful market economy.

Commonwealth control over income tax and the central bank, and central bank control over the private banks, all pillars of the postwar economy, were laid down within months of Curtin coming to office. Defended as measures required by war, which they certainly were, they endured into the peace and became more important with each passing decade. The Pacific war is now history, but the changes to the Australian political fabric made during it are as important today as they were then. The Hawke, Keating and Howard Governments were still making decisions about the role of the central bank half a century later. Paul Keating's insistence on maintaining the dominant role of the Commonwealth in income tax was the issue he used to cripple Bob Hawke in the months before Keating's second leadership challenge in 1991. As Keating said then, uniform income tax is the centre of Commonwealth power, the substance of its fiscal policy effectiveness, the agency that created the dominance of the Commonwealth over the States; an enduring legacy of John Curtin, and one that in turn is responsible for Australia's unity of purpose and internal cohesion as a small player in the modern global economy.

Since European settlement in the late eighteenth century Australia's economic success very largely depended on economies elsewhere. Through the nineteenth century and into the early twentieth, foreign capital accounted for a larger share of Australian investment, and foreign trade a larger share of production and consumption than it does today. Australia's nineteenth century prosperity was based on the expansion of the export pastoral and gold mining industries, and the high immigration and national development spending that went with them. The deterioration in prosperity that began around the time of Curtin's birth was partly caused by a global economic downturn, while the subsequent world war and Depression that formed the political and economic background to his adult years crippled the global economy. Curtin's economic commentary and analysis over those decades was often about events and trends in the global economy. One of the great issues during World War II was thus the terms on which the global economy would be reconstructed when the war had ended. Australia had a vital interest in seeing a thriving world economy, with minimum barriers to Australian exports and unhindered freedom to seek investment from abroad.

Though Australia was now at war with a powerful nearby enemy and a multitude of immediate problems pressed on his time, on appointment to office Curtin was almost immediately drawn into discussions on the shape of the postwar global economy, and Australia's place in it. The most celebrated engagement of the Chifley Government with the global institutions created in and after World War II was in the foundation of the United Nations. We know it best because Australian External Affairs minister Bert Evatt was the president of the UN General Assembly from September 1948 to May 1949.

Far more important for the postwar Australian economy, however, were the institutions that re-established a global economy after two world wars and the Depression—the IMF, the World Bank and GATT. The terms and circumstances of Australia's place in these bodies was largely decided within the frame of the Curtin and Chifley Governments, and most of the actual negotiation over the IMF and World Bank occurred while Curtin was Prime Minister. The relevant cables were addressed to or copied to Curtin, and many of the key reports from the Australian representatives in London, Stanley Bruce and Earl Page, and Australia's official representatives to the Allied financial talks in Atlantic City and Bretton Woods in the United States were directed to Curtin himself, sometimes for himself alone. Though the address was formal it meant that Curtin's advisers were kept informed of the issues, and that from time to time Curtin himself would be involved.

Australia's participation in the institutions of the global economy was thus set up by these Labor governments, and a great deal of it while Curtin was Prime Minister. The issues of Australia's attitude towards and influence over economic globalisation that continue to play a major part in Australian politics today were issues with which Curtin first grappled soon after he became Prime Minister.

Planning for Australia's place in the postwar global economy had begun in F&E under the Menzies Government in 1941, and was re-focused under the Curtin Government from February 1942. The key to the discussions in both Australia and the United Kingdom was article VII of the Mutual Aid Agreement with the United States. The article required as a condition for aid action by Britain and the United States and like-minded countries to expand trade and production and to reduce tariffs and other barriers. It was aimed squarely at the British system of imperial preference, which discriminated against US products, but it was also the basis for Allied negotiations over the rules for the postwar global economy.

In February 1942, when Curtin over-ruled Churchill on the destination of the 7th and announced the National

Economic Plan, the War Cabinet accepted that the progressive elimination of imperial preference need not stand in the way of acceptance of the Mutual Aid Agreement. This opened the way for Australia to participate in the negotiations soon to begin in England and the United States. Australian agreement was reluctant because both the Government and its advisers recognised that the United States and the United Kingdom wanted to drive down protection against imports of manufactured goods. The Curtin Government and its economic advisers believed strongly that Australia's infant manufacturing industries needed tariff protection against imports from the United Kingdom and the United States, or Australia would be merely a pastoral and service economy, unable to support a larger population and therefore unable to defend itself. Only a few economists, such as Shann in Western Australia, opposed tariff protection for Australian industry and it would be another twenty years (when manufacturing had considerably expanded) before opinion began to swing the other way. The Commonwealth Bank's chief economist Leslie Melville, who led Australia's negotiating team to the conferences that set up the IMF and the World Bank, believed in February 1943 that proposed tariff reductions were attempts to return to the 'liberal internationalism' of the late nineteenth century, which they certainly and explicitly were. To Melville 'liberal internationalism' meant Australia would not be able to impose tariffs and it would therefore, he thought, be inconsistent with full employment. To him the choice was full employment, or tariff cuts. Giblin and Coombs agreed. Australian economists widely agreed that Australian manufacturing industry was in its infancy and would need protection for many decades to come.

These views, which the Government shared, made Australia's role in the negotiations over the IMF, the World Bank and what became GATT particularly awkward. Australia saw itself as a 'developing' economy with a balance of payments constraint, and was thus keenly interested in British proposals for an international monetary fund that could make loans to members. But as a developing economy it wanted to protect its manufacturing industry. Its advisers also believed that if Australia alone pursued full employment and the rest of the world did not, Australia would see imports rising much faster than exports and the balance of payments deteriorating. It thus wanted the negotiations to succeed, but it did not want to give up the option of high and quite possibly increased protection for Australian manufacturing.

By early 1943 advisers in the Financial and Economic Committee had hit on a widely agreed though disingenuous bargaining position for the Allied negotiations on a new world economic order, a position that might protect Australia's conflicting objectives. They would demand a global commitment to full employment, as well as increased trade. This effectively meant that the United States and the United Kingdom would maintain the highest possible level of demand. Australia argued that this would sustain demand for commodity exports, at a time when tariff cuts were affecting manufacturing. If it were not accepted—and there was never a chance it would be—Australia would surely be excused from exposing its new manufacturing industry to international competition. The framework thus supported Australian manufacturing ambitions, and the traditional commodity exports—the twin goals that would remain Australia's guiding principle in trade negotiations for another 40 years.

In practice Australia's position was so transparently self-interested it was difficult to argue. The demand for a global commitment to full employment was a radical policy from a small player and it was firmly rejected by the United States. Keynes found the Australians more Keynesian than he was himself. Writing to T.S. Eliot in April 1945 he recalled that, 'Not long ago I was at a conference where the Australians urged that all the Powers in the world should sign an international compact in which each undertook to maintain full employment in their own country. I objected on the ground that this was promising to be "not only good but clever"'. Curtin's Cabinet was, anyway, seriously divided on the implications of this new international economic order, and his key advisers remained suspicious of 'liberal internationalism'. At both the preliminary Atlantic City and then the Bretton Woods meetings of 1944, Australia sent a four-man delegation. It was too small, and without the weight of a minister to make binding decisions it could have little authority. It was also constrained by disputes within Cabinet. By 1944 American and English officials were noticing a wider gap between Australia's advocacy of a global full employment policy and its unwillingness to make any commitment to liberalise its own trade barriers.

Writing to Curtin on 26 August 1944 Leslie Melville, the leader of the Australian Bretton Woods delegation, reported that he was convinced as a result of his experience that no country would play an effective role in a conference of that kind unless it had a large and strong delegation— which Australia did not. It also had trouble, Melville noted, convincing delegates of its bona fides on the full employment policy.

Curtin remained interested in the negotiations, though it is now difficult to pick up the evidence of his direct involvement. Though Melville addressed his letters to the Prime Minister, he recalled during an interview in November 2001 that this was a matter of protocol and he did not recall any direct discussions with Curtin on the issues involved. 'The issues were dealt with informally,' he said. 'F&E did work' on the IMF and World Bank negotiation and 'our drafts went to Curtin and Chifley, and we got some feedback. Curtin took more interest in them'. He recalled that Curtin 'left all the mundane things to Chifley but he took quite a part in the policy' and that 'certainly Curtin had more interest. Chifley was mainly financial in the sense of budgets and accounts. Curtin was more interested in F&E'. As Melville remarked, Curtin had written a good deal about economic policy, while Chifley had not.

Coming from Western Australia, influenced perhaps by Shann's vehemently anti-tariff views, Curtin was markedly more liberal on tariff issues than most of his Labor colleagues. The trade-off of lower tariffs in Australia for better access to other countries may have been easier for him to make. He was to say in February 1945 that:

> The Government intends to adhere to the policy of adequately protecting industries which are reasonably assured of sound opportunities of success, which assist the diversification of our economy, contribute to employment, and raise the standard of living of the community. At the same time, Australia must play her part in promoting world trade and improving economic relations. Our policy must be consistent with our international obligations. Some industries have grown up in special circumstances during the war with excessively high costs. It would be wasteful and unreasonable to seek to maintain all industries of this type.

Curtin was not present at some of the key Cabinet discussions of the Atlantic City and Bretton Woods meetings, since he was visiting the United Kingdom and North America. Illness may have prevented him making an effective contribution to a key Cabinet meeting in August 1944, when Evatt and Chifley failed to win approval for Australia's early entry to the IMF. Indeed, this may have been the whole problem with the delay in Australia's accession. Chifley tabled the Bretton Woods agreement in September 1944, the beginning of what would be a long and difficult political battle within the Labor Party to win consent to Australian membership of the new institutions. Cabinet did not approve membership until 19 November 1946, following the election in September. Opposition continued in the Caucus and party State branches, and it was not until 6 March 1947 that Chifley was able to win Caucus approval for Australia's membership. Australia accepted the articles of agreement for the World Bank and the IMF on 5 August 1947, and GATT on 13 November.

The policies on global economic issues devised by the Curtin Government in 1942 and 1943 were difficult and not entirely satisfactory, but they would remain the basic policies of Australian governments for another 40 years. Australia wanted other countries to lower barriers to Australian exports, and to support a global system of managed but flexible exchange rates backed by loans to support temporary imbalances. It wanted to share in running these institutions, despite its small economic weight. But it also wanted the freedom to protect its own manufacturing industries, and to adjust its own exchange rate if it saw fit. It was not a logical or easily defended position. As it happened, however, Australia got away with it. Its own manufacturing tariffs progressively increased after the war, while those of Europe and the United States fell.

8

Curtin in the
Australian Story

Curtin was Prime Minister for fewer than four years, yet those years rank as the most important in the history of Australia not only in organising for war, in insisting on the return of Australia's divisions, and in steadying the nation at a time of peril, but also in determining the shape of Australia's politics and economy for the following half century.

There is no doubt that Curtin's decision to direct the leading elements of the 7th Division to Australia rather than to Rangoon was in Australia's interests. There is also no doubt it marked a change in Australia's political relationship with the United Kingdom. So, too, the tilt toward the United States at the end of 1941 marked a change in Australia's international orientation. But the drama of those decisions has obscured Curtin's role in creating the institutions and the policies that determined the character of postwar Australia.

Remembering the futility of the Labor Government of the Depression as it struggled against a hostile Senate, uncooperative State governments and antagonistic business leaders, remembering the policy changes required then and refused by Labor's opponents, Curtin came to the leadership of the Labor Party determined never to be ineffectual in office, and determined to carry out the policy changes Labor had sought in the Depression. The war against Japan offered him the opportunity to do both. Roosevelt remade the US economy before World War II. Atlee remade the British economy after it. Curtin remade the Australian economy during it. If there was, as Paul Kelly argues, an Australian Settlement at Federation that included tariff protection, White Australia and wage arbitration, there was a quite new construction introduced 40 years later by the Curtin Government. It was based on Commonwealth control over monetary policy, Commonwealth control over fiscal policy and Australian engagement in a rules-based system of global trade and finance—all in pursuit of a goal of full employment. White Australia would be gone by the 1970s, and there were only remnants of tariff protection and wage arbitration by the early 1990s. But the Commonwealth's control of monetary and fiscal policy and their deployment to maintain high employment remains the unquestioned pillar of economic policy, while Australia's engagement in the institutions of the global economy remains as important as it did in the first postwar decades. As Butlin and Schedvin wrote in *War Economy*:

By the end of the war Australia's economic institutions
and administrative arrangements were to be transformed
beyond recognition . . . but the change which was to
be of the greatest long term significance was to be the
realization that the economic system could be
administered in such a way as to provide continuous
employment for the vast majority of the working
population.

The Curtin Government provided not only the goal but
also the means.

Curtin held the office of Prime Minister for three years
and nine months, and crowded most of his great
achievements into the first two and a half years. Don
Rodgers recalled that Curtin was never himself after his
return from the United Kingdom and North America in
July 1944. He suffered his first heart attack in November
that year, returned to work, then died in the Lodge after
a prolonged illness at the beginning of July 1945. He had
lived to see Germany surrender in May, and died just six
weeks before the surrender of Japan.

So short a time in office, but Australians knew what he
had accomplished and what it meant for them. The morning
of Curtin's funeral in Perth was bright and sunny. There
had already been a half-hour funeral service in King's Hall,
Parliament House, attended by ministers, ambassadors and
the Australian service chiefs before the plane bearing
Curtin's body left Canberra Airport. Training with his
high school football team, Clive Harvie's coach asked

them to stand to attention, a line of fifteen boys stretched across the school oval looking up at the plane flying low, coming from the northeast over Mount Ainslie and the Civic shops. As a young ministerial staffer, Jim Maher was sometimes taken by Curtin to the Australian Rules game on a Saturday at Manuka Oval. 'It will keep you out of trouble, Jim,' Curtin told him. Now Maher joined other young people from ministerial offices on the roof to watch the plane carrying the coffin to Perth circle Parliament House one last time. In Western Australia, thousands crowded the Fremantle railway station, trying to get a train to the cemetery at Karrakatta. It was the first fine day for six weeks. Mourners lined both sides of the streets to the cemetery. The sandflies were bad in Perth in July: they bothered young Eunice Lee, waiting with her family in Loch Street for the funeral procession to pass by to Karrakatta, where more than 20 000 people waited in the bright sunshine. From a tiny mortuary near his home in Cottesloe, Curtin's coffin was carried by on a gun carriage heaped with red carnations.

Notes

1 Sleepless Vigil

'pacing the grounds of the Lodge': F.C. Green, *Servant of The House*, Heinemann, Sydney, 1969, p. 128. See also John Curtin Prime Ministerial Library (JCPML), Records of the Curtin family; J. Thompson, *John Curtin: Portrait of a Prime Minister*, JCPML00406/9, May 1959.

'should Japan reach the national capital': JCPML, Records of Tom Fitzgerald. Notes *re* conversation with F.T. Smith, 15–18 February 1985, JCPML00653/513/5.

'ten pounds over his normal weight': JCPML, Records of Hector Harrison. Note from F. McLaughlin to Hector Harrison and biographical notes *re* John Curtin 1945, JCPML00472/4.

'invade Australia if she so desires': D. Horner, *Defence Supremo*, Allen & Unwin, Sydney, p. 139.

'landing on the east coast by May': P. Stanley, *Australia Under Threat of Invasion*, Australian War Memorial, Canberra 2002. Referenced to A5954, 563/1 5 March 1942, National Archives of Australia.

'on the night of 3 October 1941': the Government was sworn in on 7 October.

'did not leave until midnight': D. Rodgers, oral history, JCPML, Records of the National Library of Australia, 1971, JCPML00497/1.

'of course he couldn't': author's interview with Elsie. See also JCPML, Interview with Elsie MacLeod, 10/05/1994– 20/02/1995, JCPML00012/1.

'a straight-on appearance': JCPML, Records of the National Library of Australia. Interview of Donald K. Rodgers, 1971, JCPML00497/1.

'Kruschen Salts': JCPML, Records of Tom Fitzgerald. Notes *re* conversation with Elsie MacLeod, 29 April 1984, JCPML00653/215/4.

'in the words of a newspaper obituary': D. Black, *In His Own Words: John Curtin's Speeches and Writings*, Paradigm Books, Curtin University, Perth 1995, quoted on the back cover.

'a mediocre . . . peacetime Prime Minister': S. Macintyre, *The Australian*, 5 July 1995.

'a fortunate . . . man': D. Black, *In His Own Words*, p. xii.

'greater than his intrinsic qualities': F. Alexander, *Australia Since Federation*, Nelson, Melbourne, 1974, p. 169.

'the vision for postwar Australia': D. Day, *Chifley: A Life*, Harper Collins, Sydney, 2001, p. 1.

2 Saint Jack

'in his history of . . . Parliament': G. Souter, *Acts of Parliament*, Melbourne University Press, Melbourne, 1988, p. 343.

'Alan Fraser claimed': J. Thompson, *John Curtin: Portrait of a Prime Minister*, JCPML00406/9.

'**who never sought office**': JCPML, Records of Hector Harrison. Note from F. McLaughlin to Hector Harrison and biographical notes *re* John Curtin, 1945, JCPML00472/4.

'**her birthday gift**': D. Black, *Friendship is a Sheltering Tree: John Curtin's letters 1907–1945*, JCPML, 2001, p. 207.

'**if it meant filling a lesser role**': JCPML, Records of Tom Fitzgerald. Letter from Elsie MacLeod to Tom Fitzgerald, 6 October 1989, JCPML00705/1/24. (Elsie MacLeod tells a different story in JCPML00705/1/121. The position for Curtin looked so acute that the Labor member for Hunter in New South Wales, Mr R. James, offered to stand down in his seat for Curtin. Curtin stated that 'Mr James is too valuable a man to be lost to Parliament. His services are needed in Parliament as well as anybody else's'.)

'**to accept the responsibility of power**': I. Young, *Theodore: His Life and Times*, Alpha Books, Sydney, 1971, p. 171. Young suggests Evatt's plotting continued after Curtin become Prime Minister. Shortly after Japan entered the war, Evatt invited Theodore to a meeting to discuss the formation of national Government. According to Young, 'Theodore showed no further interest when it became apparent Evatt would be leader'.

'**keeping Labor's frontbenchers from the ministry**': J. Griffin, *John Wren: A Life Reconsidered*, Scribe, Melbourne, p. 287.

'**alliance with other parties**': D. Black, *In His Own Words*, p. 7.

'**insist on no alliance being made**': ibid., p. 19.

'**any coalition with the Nationals**': Curtin parried Menzies' proposal for a coalition by suggesting in October the creation of an Advisory War Council with Government and Opposition leaders as members. It informed Opposition members about the war and Australian readiness, and prepared its leaders for office. In the event Curtin had only a year to wait from the election at the end of September 1940 to the collapse of the Menzies and then Fadden Governments.

'Curtin has privately made it clear': Menzies to Bruce, 11 September 1939, NAA: Personal Papers of Prime Minister Bruce, M103 1938/39 (Supplementary war file 1938–39).

'pointing out Menzies' meagre results': in the same letter to Bruce, Menzies suggested it wasn't too late for the British to call off the war by doing a deal with Hitler over Poland. With Hitler—as, perhaps, with Curtin—Menzies took some claims at face value and believed what he wanted to believe.

'who understood and shared the fears': JCPML, Records of Lynette Finch; L. Finch, *Revealing Unsuspected Powers of Leadership: Analyzing the Myth of John Curtin*, 1999, JCPML00639/1.

'as one writer argues': ibid.

'transformation of the Prime Minister's image': as Finch points out, Curtin and his press secretary Don Rodgers contributed to the changing attitudes. 'Through the use of unprecedented openness and frankness with a select group of senior journalists, Curtin bound Australia's leading political reporters into confidentiality and hence silence.'

'played up the story of Curtin's vigil': the late Richard Hall, who worked with Rodgers at the ABC, maintained that this is exactly what Rodgers did. Hall, pers. comm.

'alternating with spells of exhilaration': Hall, pers. comm.

'a crying drunk': JCPML, Records of the National Library of Australia. Interview with Donald K. Rodgers, 1971, JCPML00497/1.

'his account of the Depression': J.T. Lang, *The Great Bust*, McNamara's Books, Leura, 1980.

'he told reporters': C. Lloyd and R. Hall, *Backroom Briefings: John Curtin's War*, National Library of Australia, Canberra, 1997.

'opposed sending Australian forces overseas': Caucus minutes quoted by H.C. Coombs, 14th John Curtin Memorial Lecture, Australian National University, 14 November 1984.

'it is a White Australia': Australia Day 1942 national broadcast, *Digest of Decisions and Announcements and Important Speeches by The Prime Minister (The Hon. John Curtin)*, no. 16, 19 January 1942–28 January 1942.

3 Bringing the Troops Home

'a few premonitory disputes': he disagreed with the British Prime Minister almost immediately over the relief of Australian troops in Tobruk and a little later over a suggestion that Australian troops might be used in a campaign in Turkey.

'defeat the Soviet Union': the Soviet Union had held the German invasion by the winter of 1941, but the battle of Stalingrad would not begin until July 1942 and it would be November before the Soviet Union counter-attacked and trapped General Paulus' Sixth Army in what was later seen as a turning point of World War II.

'ground to powder': W.S. Churchill, *The Second World War, Volume 3: The Grand Alliance*, Cassell, London, 1949, p. 539.

'its navies would control the Mediterranean': Churchill's view was widely shared. Dr van Mook, the Lieutenant Governor General of the Netherlands East Indies, told the Australian Advisory War Council just after the fall of Singapore that 'once the Netherlands East Indies were reduced, the Japanese would not be likely to embark on a large scale invasion of Australia, but instead they would concentrate their forces on assisting the Germans in the Middle East and attacking Russia through Manchukuo. This would seriously endanger the Allied position in Europe and would prolong the war for a very long period'. Advisory War Council meeting, 18 February 1942.

'the Japanese threat to the British Far East base': G.H. Gill, *The Royal Australian Navy 1939–1942*, Australian War Memorial, Canberra, 1957, p. 562.

'the United States would assume responsibility for Australia': like so much else in the relationship between Australia and the United States, the Pacific alliance was part of the higher alliance between the United States and the United Kingdom. The same would later be true of the intelligence relationship and, in the next century, would find echoes in Australia's commitment to the US–UK invasion of Iraq in 2003.

'Churchill proposed': F. Shedden, *Victory Under the Curtin and Chifley Governments* (MS), Chapter 9, Australian Archives CRS A5954 (boxes 1320–1327).

'relying on the British fleet': Japan had not always been regarded as a probable enemy. As an ally in 1914 the Japanese navy had convoyed Australian troops from Western Australia to the Middle East. L. Carlyon, *Gallipoli*, Pan Macmillan, Sydney, 2001, p. 121.

'an impregnable Singapore base': Shedden MS, 'Introduction'. The idea had been expressed by the First Lord of the Admiralty as early as the Imperial Conference of 1909, but it was not until the last months of 1941 that Britain based a fleet of capital ships in Singapore, by which time it was vulnerable to air attack. Within Australia the Singapore strategy was supported by the Navy, but the Army queried Singapore's impregnability and Australian reliance on the British fleet.

'his priorities, he later wrote': W.S. Churchill, *The Second World War, Volume 3: The Grand Alliance*, p. 523.

'Churchill cabled Curtin': Shedden MS, Chapter 6.

'during an Australian Advisory War Council meeting': Shedden MS, Chapter 4.

'it had always been the intention': Menzies told Duff Cooper that 'Churchill had always told him of the importance which he attached to the defence of Singapore, but he doubted if Churchill was, in fact, fully seized with its vital significance'.

'that could catch and kill anything': Shedden MS, Chapter 6.

'an Empire Defence strategy based on Singapore': Curtin's alarm may have been encouraged by Shedden, who had consistently opposed the Army view in favour of the Empire Defence view and was thus obliged to inflate the importance of the Singapore base.

'a war against Japan': In talks with the UK before Pearl Harbor the US was not convinced that the loss of Malaya would have a decisive effect on the issue of the war.

'loss of strategic advantage': on 5 March Churchill telegraphed Roosevelt that 'We have suffered the greatest disaster in our history at Singapore' (W.S. Churchill, *The Second World War, Volume 4: The Hinge of Fate*, p. 169), not because Japan's possession of the city mattered so very much to the war, but because the Allied defeat was in Churchill's view so dishonourable. Australians are said to celebrate defeats, but prefer gallant defeats such as the Dardanelles campaign. The anniversary of the surrender of Singapore, a more important defeat, is not widely marked.

'Major General Gordon Bennett': Shedden MS, Chapter 12.

'from Palestine to Singapore': W.S. Churchill, *The Second World War, Volume 3: The Grand Alliance*, p. 565.

'be moved to Singapore': D. Horner, *Defence Supremo*, p. 133.

'to Malaya, or directly to Singapore': Advisory War Council, 31 December 1941 (Melbourne meeting). The cable mentioned that Churchill had wirelessed this to London for Curtin one week earlier.

'the Advisory War Council': Advisory War Council, 5 January 1942. The decision was taken subsequently as the decision of the War Cabinet.

'left Port Tewfik, Egypt': J. Warby, *The 25 Pounders*, 2/6 Field Regiment Association, 1995, pp. 144–5.

'**one private recalled**': the author's father-in-law, the late Bob Hope. Then known as 'Padder' Hope, he was a young private in the 2/6th Field Regiment of the Royal Australian Artillery.

'**a man's territory was his bed**': J. Warby, *The 25 Pounders*.

'**Java and Sumatra could not be held**': this section relies on D. Horner, *Inside the War Cabinet*, Allen & Unwin, Sydney, 1996.

'**not the place to make a stand**': Wavell advised Curtin the same day that the odds against a successful defence in the NEI were mounting, and suggested the Australians be diverted to either Burma or Australia.

'**for a meeting in Sydney**': Full Cabinet, 17 February 1942.

'**divert the 7th Division to Burma**': non-Government members' views in favour of Burma are recorded in the Advisory War Council record for the meeting of 19 February 1942, chaired by Forde in Curtin's absence. D. Horner, *Inside the War Cabinet*, Chapter 10.

'**21 days to re-sort their equipment**': Advisory War Council, 24 February 1942.

'**the only sensible decision**': 'undoubtedly the 7th Division would have been lost if it had landed at Rangoon', D. Horner, *Inside the War Cabinet*, p. 108.

'**ignored its military advisers**': Shedden MS, 'Introduction'.

'**had a big effect on the 1943 election**': JCPML, Records of the National Library of Australia. Interview of Donald K. Rodgers, 1971, JCPML00497/1.

4　Curtin as Warlord

'**they stayed there until mid-July**': D. McCarthy, *South-West Pacific Area—First Year*, vol. V of Series 1 (Army) of *Australia* *in the War of 1939–45*, Australian War Memorial, Canberra, 1959, p. 119.

'only four of the eleven brigades': ibid., p. 118.

'reported to MacArthur': B. Ralph, *They Passed This Way*, Kangaroo Press, Sydney, 2000, p. 94.

'there were 271 000 troops': J. Robertson, *Australia at War 1939–45*, Heinemann, Melbourne, 1981, p. 101.

'still in the Middle East': D. McCarthy, *South-West Pacific Area— First Year*, p. 189.

'The US troops swelled the numbers': the main body of the US 41st Division arrived by early April 1942.

'at any time in 1942': J. Robertson, *Australia At War 1939–45*, p. 102.

'no, at no time': D. McCarthy, *South-West Pacific Area—First Year*, p. 113.

'blockading Australia and raiding its coast': on 13 February Admiral Raeder had told Hitler that 'Rangoon, Singapore and, most likely, also Port Darwin will be in Japanese hands within a few weeks'.

'writes one historian': E. Bergerud, *Touched with Fire: The Land War in the South Pacific*, Viking, New York, 1996, p. 14.

'the Japanese had 10 000': D. McCarthy, *South-West Pacific Area—First Year*, p. 234.

'Curtin tended somewhat to exaggerate': J. Robertson, *Australia At War 1939–45*, p. 103.

'he did so deliberately': P. Stanley, *Australia Under Threat of Invasion*, Australian War Memorial, Canberra, 2002.

'changed the Pacific strategic situation': Full Cabinet, 9 June 1942.

'the danger of invasion had passed': he told Cabinet on 27 September 1943.

'Curtin beat the invasion drum': G. Harper, cited by P. Stanley, *Australia Under Threat of Invasion*, Australian War Memorial, Canberra, 2002.

'In England, Churchill also regretted': R. Jenkins, *Churchill*, Pan Books, London, 2002.

'a major counter-offensive': nor is it a powerful point to argue, as Stanley does, that the British General staff and Churchill had assured Curtin he need not fear Japanese invasion. They had also told him Japan was unlikely to come into the war, that Malaya would be held and that Singapore was secure.

'to prepare for the defeat of Japan': see Australia Day 1943 speech, *Digest of Decisions and Announcements and Important Speeches by The Prime Minister (The Hon. John Curtin)*, no. 52, 26 January 1943–11 February 1943.

'until Germany had surrendered': though Shedden and Curtin should and may have known of it earlier (the agreement was reached before Japan entered the war, as noted by Bergerud), in May 1942 External Affairs Minister Bert Evatt cabled Curtin from London reporting his discovery of a formal agreement between Churchill and Roosevelt, contemplating Germany's defeat before that of Japan. 'The existence of this written agreement came as a great surprise to myself and no doubt to you', Evatt wrote. S.L. Carruthers, *Australia under Siege: Japanese Submarine Raiders 1942*, Solus Books, Sydney, 1982, p. 48.

'at the Casablanca conference': D. Black, *In His Own Words*, Paradigm Books, Curtin University, Perth, 1995, p. 213.

'in the first year of the war': E. Bergerud, *Touched with Fire: The Land War in the South Pacific*, 1996, p. 18. The 'Germany first' agreement was made before the United States entered the war. It was thus highly sensitive because of its political implications, and it was made before Pearl Harbor and therefore before mass hostility to Japan made United States involvement necessary.

'came to the same conclusion': D. McCarthy, *South-West Pacific Area—First Years*, p. 190.

'**the most stunning and decisive blow**': J. Keegan, *The Second World War*, Pimlico, London, 1997, p. 228.

'**completely in his hands**': G. Souter, *Acts of Parliament*, Melbourne University Press, Melbourne, 1988, p. 349.

'**in March 1942**': as early as 22 December 1941 Curtin had been alerted by Casey that the United States contemplated an American commander for the Southwest Pacific and it would likely be MacArthur. Curtin responded on 23 December that Australia would 'gladly accept' a US commander in the Pacific area. Roosevelt and Churchill instead appointed Wavell. MacArthur arrived in Darwin from the Philippines in March and Curtin announced Australia's agreement to his appointment as Supreme Commander on 18 March, the day Roosevelt cabled Churchill that 'Australia must be held and we are willing to undertake that'.

'**It is difficult to find a single instance**': E. Bergerud, *Touched with Fire: The Land War in the South Pacific*, 1996, p. 250.

'**Australia had the best army**': ibid.

'**cannot be classified as attack troops**': Blamey to Curtin, 4 December 1942, D. McCarthy, *South-West Pacific Area— First Year*, pp. 449, 450.

'**Australians alone in the Southwest Pacific area**': ibid., p. 590.

'**would have strengthened his position**': Fitzgerald speculated that Curtin recognised MacArthur's intelligence and value while Chifley, who took a sceptical and deflating attitude, was not smart enough to recognise the brains behind the showmanship. JCPML, Records of Tom Fitzgerald. Notes *re* Shedden papers in the Australian Archives, December 1984, JCPML00653/208/9.

'**Curtin was fortunate**': ibid.

'**though the American people were animated**': P. Edwards, *From Curtin to Beazley: Labor Leaders and the American Alliance*, JCPML Public Lecture, 8 October 2001, JCPML00667/1. The Prime Minister's War Conference met in Melbourne on the morning of 1 June 1942. Curtin, MacArthur, Shedden and MacArthur's chief of staff, Major General Sutherland, were present.

'seek the protection of the United States': F. Shedden, *Victory under the Curtin and Chifley Governments* (MS), 'Introduction' Australian Archives CRS A5954 (boxes 1320–1327).

'when Japan attacked': Shedden MS, Chapter 10.

'if the United States entered the conflict': David Horner, 'Strategy and Command in Australia's Campaigns of 1941', 2001 History Conference, *Remembering 1941*, Australian War Memorial.

'The Australian War Cabinet accepted a US proposal': Shedden MS, Chapter 6.

'Just before the Japanese attack': 5 December 1941.

'along similar lines to Great Britain': Full Cabinet, 8 December 1941.

'Ward complained in Cabinet': Full Cabinet, 23 November 1943, archive 2703, vol. 1D—full minutes.

'when he turned toward the United States': in September 1942 he told Commonwealth Bank Governor Claude Reading he had asked for the British Eastern Fleet to come into Australian waters. C. Lloyd and R. Hall, *Backroom Briefings: John Curtin's War*, National Library of Australia, Canberra, 1997, p. 85.

'as much the King of Australia': implied change to direct quote.

5 Jack Curtin and the Social Question

'within days of his appointment': F. Shedden, *Victory Under the Curtin and Chifley Governments* (MS), Chapter 17, Australian Archives CRS A5954 (boxes 1320–1327).

'as wool prices fell': merino wool prices fell around 30 per cent from 1890 to 1894. A. Barnard, *The Australian Wool*

Market 1840–1900, Melbourne University Press, Parkville, 1958, p. 203.

'the most severe shock': R. Gollan, *The Commonwealth Bank of Australia*, Australian National University Press, Canberra, 1968, p. 27.

'before the six colonies federated': his father took him along when he went to vote for Federation, telling the boy it was a day he would remember always. JCPML, Records of Tom Fitzgerald. Letter from Fitzgerald to Mrs Kath Spehr and notes *re* conversation with Mrs Spehr, 1989, JCPML00653/214/52.

'Curtin's earliest surviving letters': D. Black, *In His Own Words*, Paradigm Books, Curtin University, Perth, 1995.

'The young Curtin': this section is greatly indebted to the unpublished work of Tom Fitzgerald, whose papers include a collection of material on the formation of Curtin's economic ideas.

'a formidable polemicist': even by his early twenties the range and depth of Curtin's reading in classical and Marxist economics were daunting. Among socialists and at that time Curtin's deep reading in economic theory was not unusual. By the 1890s, speakers and writers in the Labor movement could cite early economic writers such as Jevons, Mill, Marx, Spencer, Hobson and Ely, and know they would be recognised. See JCPML, Records of Tom Fitzgerald. C.D.W. Goodwin, *Economic Enquiry in Australia 1876–1966*, JCPML00653/156.

'correct economic laws shall prevail': Records of Tom Fitzgerald; Curtin, 'Ideals of the Labor Movement', *Daily News*, 23 June 1919, JCPML00653/226/46.

'Writing in September 1906': JCPML, Records of the Victorian Socialist Party. 'The International Spirit', *The Socialist*, 1 September 1906, pp. 5, 6. JCPML00819/2.

'Writing in **The Socialist**': JCPML, Records of Tom Fitzgerald. Notes *re* VSP activities, 1907, JCPML00653/435/2; see also 'Surplus Value', *The Socialist*, 5 January 1907, p. 2, JCPML00819/008.

'The essence of the Social Question': the 5 January Curtin piece was criticised by W.H. Emmett in the 12 January 1907 issue of *The Socialist*, evidently from a Marxist perspective. JCPML, Records of Tom Fitzgerald. Notes *re* VSP activities, 1907, JCPML00653/435/2.

'By February 1907': ibid.

'Three years later': JCPML, Records of Tom Fitzgerald. Victorian Socialist Party affairs 1910, JCPML00653/442, folio 78. See also JCPML, Records of the Victorian Socialist Party. 'At The Gaiety: A study in chaos. Mr J. Curtin Makes a Plea for Fundamental Propaganda', *The Socialist*, 22 July 1910, p. 2, JCPML00819/047.

'the Rubira Café in Bourke Street': JCPML, Records of Tom Fitzgerald. 1909–1910 (including Mann's farewell), JCPML00653/439, folios 1–5.

'of all the men who have influenced me': *Commonwealth Parliamentary Debates*, vol. 165, p. 32. Quoted in B.R. Nugent, 'Frank Anstey in Victorian Politics', MA thesis, University of New England, Armidale, 1973, JCPML00745/1.

'to the South Pacific and Asia': I. Turner, 'Anstey, Francis George', in B. Nairn and G. Serle (eds), *Australian Dictionary of Biography*, vol. 7: 1891–1939, Melbourne University Press, Melbourne, 1979, pp. 79–81.

'Curtin was elected President': B.R. Nugent, 'Frank Anstey in Victorian Politics', MA thesis, University of New England, Armidale, 1973, p. 275, note 37.

'Anstey helped him recover': ibid., p. 274.

'in the **Westralian Worker**': D. Black, *In His Own Words*, p. 1. Black gives a 1915 date, but Gollan in *The Commonwealth Bank of Australia* gives 1917.

'Ever since I have been living': JCPML, Records of Tom Fitzgerald. J. Curtin, 'The late Frank Hyett', *Railways Union Gazette*, 7 June 1919, JCPML00653/28/5.

'the early day's of Curtin's editorship': B.R. Nugent, 'Frank Anstey in Victorian Politics', MA thesis, University of New England, Armidale, 1973, JCPML00745/1, p. 275, note 44.

'It is quite impossible for me': JCPML, Records of Hugh Mahon. Note from John Curtin to Hugh Mahon thanking him for his generosity, 9 February 1917, JCPML00480/1.

'for the next twelve years': the Australian Workers' Union took control of the paper in 1919, obliging some changes in Curtin's radical editorial stance. D. Day, *Chifley*, Harper Collins, Sydney, 2001, p. 263.

'the year after the war ended': JCPML, Records of Tom Fitzgerald. J. Curtin, 'Ideals of the Labor Movement', *Daily News*, 23 June 1919, JCPML00653/226/46.

'a June 1917 speech': JCPML, Records of Tom Fitzgerald. Notes *re* War and Economics, 1917, JCPML00653/132/8.

'newly published works': including a book by English neo-classical economist Pigou in 1920 and D.A. Baker's *Cash and Credit* the following year.

'Revision of the Treaty': JCPML, Records of Tom Fitzgerald. Notes *re* Curtin and economics, 1903–1931, JCPML00653/131/9. Curtin refers to all three books in a 1924 editorial. JCPML, Records of the Australian Labor Party, WA Branch. *Westralian Worker* editorial, 29 February 1924, JCPML00302/365.

'*Economic Consequences of the Peace*': 31 March 1925.

'He would later write': on 30 December 1932.

'no more interesting person': Fitzgerald believed Curtin had read every significant work of Keynes up to and including the 1930 *Treatise on Money*.

6   Jack Curtin MHR and the Great Depression

'the chief figure in defeating me': Curtin to his wife, 9 July 1930, in D. Black, *Friendship is a Sheltering Tree: John Curtin's Letters 1907–1945*, JCPML, 2001, p. 145.

'kept him out of the ministry': W. Denning, *Caucus Crisis*, Hale & Iremonger, Sydney, 1982 [1937], p. 114.

'the mines at Broken Hill': N. Cain, 'Theodore, Edward Granville', in J. Ritchie (ed.), *Australian Dictionary of Biography*, vol. 12: 1891–1939, Melbourne University Press, Melbourne, pp. 197–202.

'organised in secret': W. Denning, *Caucus Crisis*, p. 24.

'principally in London': B. Dyster and D. Meredith, *Australia in the International Economy*, Cambridge University Press, 1990, Chapter 6, pp. 131–2.

'a net outflow': ibid.

'from a Notes Board to the Bank': L.F. Giblin, *The Growth of a Central Bank*, Melbourne University Press, Melbourne, 1951, p. 1.

'beyond the end of November': L. Ross, *John Curtin: A Biography*, Sun Books, Melbourne, 1983, pp. 103, 104.

'Six months later': 10 June 1930.

'In 1930 he published': JCPML, Records of John Curtin. *Australia's economic crisis and the £55,000,000 Interest Bill*, JCPML00593/1.

'interest payments on debt in sterling': the trading banks were nonetheless obliged to announce a devaluation on 10 March 1930. It also depreciated against the rest of the world when the UK dropped the gold standard and depreciated against the US dollar.

'by devaluation elsewhere': Keynes' article is reprinted in L.J. Louis and I. Turner, *The Depression of the 1930s*, Cassell, Melbourne, 1968, pp. 218–22.

'In early July': Theodore resigned on 9 July.

'the States and the Commonwealth': R. Fitzgerald, *Red Ted: The Life of E.G. Theodore*, University of Queensland Press, Brisbane, 1994, p. 278.

'At the end of August': Scullin was too ill to attend the meetings, and Lyons acted for him.

'Anstey was well to the left': I. Turner, 'Anstey, Francis George', in B. Nairn and G. Serle, *Australian Dictionary of Biography*, vol. 7: 1891–1939, p. 80.

'meeting as the Loan Council': R. Fitzgerald, *Red Ted: The Life of E.G. Theodore*, p. 278.

'Curtin moved': Caucus Minutes, 6 August 1930.

'outstripped the means of exchange': Curtin was still in a sense an under-consumptionist, but the cause of the problem had shifted from declining wages to insufficient credit.

'not be implemented in Australia': other than a brief and unsatisfactory experience for the years 1920–1924, when the money supply was tightly restricted and the exchange rate allowed to appreciate. W. Coleman, 'A brief history of the Australian Notes Issue Board 1920–1924', *Cato Journal*, vol. 19, no. 1, Spring/Summer, 1999.

'I would ask this Parliament': one of the stronger views Curtin held during the great debates of the Depression was that Australia should depreciate its currency against sterling. This was strongly opposed by the Commonwealth Bank board chairman Sir Robert Gibson, and by the banks generally. Australia did depreciate (without Gibson's blessing) in 1931. Curtin understood that credit creation in Australia was limited so long as the Australian pound could be freely converted to sterling at a fixed exchange rate. The fixed exchange rate meant the quantity of Australian pounds had to be related to the quantity of sterling and gold held as reserves.

'increasing the note issue': or the monetary base or high-powered money, as the monetarists would have said in the 1970s and 1980s.

'Mr Curtin is probably the finest speaker': W. Denning, *Caucus Crisis*, p. 51.

'in January 1931': 6 January.

'and three weeks later': 29 January.

'by early March': 6 March.

'Opposition Leader John Latham': Latham scoffed at proposals to allow the Commonwealth Bank to create money.

'both were deeply influenced': Theodore had copies of Keynes' books—sent by mining executive W.S. Robinson, according to Melville. JCPML, Records of the National Library of Australia. Interview with Sir Leslie Melville, 3 January 1973, JCPML00714/1.

'similar economic views': Theodore was opposed to a flexible exchange rate, which was one point of difference.

'according to Denning': W. Denning, *Caucus Crisis*, p. 148.

'Green thought Anstey': F.C. Green, *Servant of The House*, Heinemann, Sydney, 1969, p. 42.

'in return for continued bank funding': the Labor Party Executive had declared hostility to parts of the plan and allowed a free vote to Members of Parliament.

'Curtin's drinking problems': JCPML, Records of Tom Fitzgerald. Notes *re* conversation with Angus McLachlan, 30 April 1984, JCPML00687/14/29

'Curtin wrote to him': 30 September 1932. JCPML, Records of Lloyd Ross; Anstey Curtin notes, correspondence and cuttings, 1924–1932, JCPML00301/1.

'In an answering letter': 14 November 1932.

'royal commission into the banking system': D. Day, *Chifley: A Life*, Harper Collins, Sydney, 2001, p. 342.

'an issue of administrative effectiveness': D. Black, *In His Own Words*, Paradigm Books, Curtin University, Perth, 1995, pp. 132–4.

'the lessons of the Depression': JCPML, Records of Tom Fitzgerald. Notes *re* articles in *Westralian Worker*, 22 October 1937 and *The Wheatgrower*, 3 June 1937, JCPML00653/226/44.

'Responding to the July 1937 Report': JCPML, Records of Tom Fitzgerald. 'Labor and the Commonwealth Bank', *Westralian Worker*, 22 October 1937, JCPML00653/226/42.

'wages and working conditions': W. Denning, *Caucus Crisis*, p. 89.

'excessive and unintelligent protection': ibid., p. 148.

'easy familiarity with concepts and numbers': the speech was given on 12 September 1939. Commonwealth Parliamentary Debates, vols 161–179, 21 September 1939–17 July 1944.

'in January 1941': Budget debate, 6 January 1941.

7 Prime Minister Curtin Changes Australia

'introduced the Budget': *Digest of Decisions and Announcements and Important Speeches by The Prime Minister (The Hon. John Curtin)*, no. 3, 29 October 1941–3 November 1941.

'efficiently and without question': F. Shedden, *Victory Under the Curtin and Chifley Governments* (MS), Chapter 17, Australian Archives CRS A5954 (boxes 1320–1327).

'economic adjustments that might be expected': quoted in H.C. Coombs, *Curtin: A Consensus Prime Minister?*, Australian National University lecture, Canberra, 1984, JCPML00419/8.

'a fairer distribution of wealth': ibid.

'autonomy within their areas': S.J. Butlin and C.B. Schedvin, *The War Economy 1942–1945*, Australian War Memorial, Canberra, 1997, p. 10.

'presided over by the Treasurer': Full Cabinet, 17 February 1942. Full Cabinet was to function 'as heretofore'.

'Outlining the Budget proposals': Full Cabinet on 7 July 1942.

'the funeral of so many economic theories': L.F. Giblin, *The Growth of a Central Bank,* Melbourne University Press, Melbourne, 1951, p. 298.

'the principles of postwar reconstruction': H.C. Coombs, *Curtin: A Consensus Prime Minister?,* JCPML00419/8.

'he was an abler man': JCPML, Records of the National Library of Australia. Interview with Sir Leslie Melville, 3 January 1973, JCPML00714/1.

'a deeper interest': Melville, pers. comm.

'Ten days after the new Government was sworn in': Full Cabinet, 17 October 17 1941.

'the Commonwealth Bank': at this 17 October meeting Cabinet discussed the makeup of the board and the policy of the Commonwealth Bank, but no details are in the record.

'Chifley told Cabinet': Full Cabinet, 18 October 1941.

'Curtin and Chifley discussed': Chifley briefed Cabinet on the discussion, then read part of the text of his Budget speech to be given two days later. See Full Cabinet, 27 October 1941.

'were quite determined': RBA Archives Conference with trading banks, Sydney, 27 October 1941.

'One banker asked': Mr McConnan.

'to disallow the regulation': this last sentence has an editing line through it.

'the dangers in the Government's policy': Mr Healy.

'a revolutionary change in the position': S.J. Butlin, *War Economy 1939–1942*, Australian War Memorial, Canberra, 1955, p. 394.

'the **Commonwealth Constitution**': L.F. Giblin, *The Growth of a Central Bank*, p. 285.

'**Leslie Melville in Melbourne**': RBA Archives—Conference, Melbourne, 8 December 1941.

'**central bank credit creation**': on 12 February Reading wrote to Chifley complaining of the 'expansion of credit much greater than was contemplated in the Budget' and urging the need for 'corrective action', including rationing. On 25 April Armitage told Chifley rationing did not go far enough and should be extended to a large range of goods 'to prevent the orgy of spending [that] is at present going on, and direct the moneys into War Loans'.

'**the 1942–43 Budget**': the Bank drew up a memo showing the increase in Treasury Bills of £33 million pounds in 1941–42 and estimating a shortfall in 1942–43 of £130 million. It concluded 'The Board would like to know by what means the Government proposes to cover the gap'. Reading requested a meeting with the Prime Minister and Chifley, given Curtin's public statements that war expenditure for 1942–43 would not be less than £400 million and there would be no increase in direct or indirect taxation. Chifley arranged a meeting in Canberra on 3 July.

'**Armitage's notes of the meeting**': RBA Archives—Memorandum Discussion with the Prime Minister and the Treasurer, 3 July 1942.

'**the Commonwealth's authority**': Full Cabinet, 17 February 1942.

'**and one year afterward**': JE34 Digest 26, Uniform income tax— Curtin speech to Premiers' Conference, 22 April 1942. Chifley in a separate statement refers to 'after the war' when 'we revert to the former method of dual taxation', and adds, 'May I say that, whether in peace or in war, I have little liking for that system'. *Digest of Decisions and Announcements and Important Speeches by The Prime*

Minister (The Hon. John Curtin), no. 26, 15 April 1942–27
April 1942.

'impose uniform taxation': *Digest of Decisions and Announcements
and Important Speeches by The Prime Minister (The Hon.
John Curtin)*, no. 28.

'NSW Labor Premier Bill McKell': E.G. Whitlam, Chifley Memorial
Dinner, 7 September 1991.

'for specific purposes': T.H. Kewley, *Australian Social Security
Today: Major Developments from 1900 to 1978*, Sydney
University Press, 1980, p. 29. Jill Roe also made the point.
I am indebted to David Black for emphasising the
connection between uniform taxation and the expansion
of Commonwealth social security.

'never go back on that principle': from *A Place Apart: The Official
History of the University of Melbourne*, Melbourne University
Press, 1996, cited by E.G. Whitlam in a 13 June 2002
speech.

'National Welfare Scheme': T.H. Kewley, *Australian Social Security
Today: Major Developments from 1900 to 1978*, pp. 29ff.

'in October 1943': 20 October 1943.

'the following month': Full Cabinet, 23 November 1943.

'On 29 April 1942': S. Cornish, *Full Employment in Australia: The
Genesis of a White Paper* Department of Economic History,
Faculty of Economics, Australian National University,
Canberra, 1987, p. 8.

'opportunities for such employment': ibid., p. 11.

'The origins ... are now obscure': Cornish writes that it is uncertain
'whether the initiative in Australia to prepare a white paper
on employment policy lay with the politicians or with their
public service advisers'. Coombs claimed that a statement
on postwar employment policy had been in preparation since
1943, when the Ministry of Post War Reconstruction was
established—and that the idea went back to a conference
of economists in Canberra in 1938. The British full

employment paper that was the model was tabled 27 May 1944. As early as 11 May 1944, N.G. Butlin at the Australian High Commission in London had informed Coombs of the imminent release of the paper and on 30 May sent two copies to Coombs.

'recently published in the UK': S.J. Butlin and C.B. Schedvin, *True War Economy 1942–1945*, Australian War Memorial, Canberra, 1997, p. 673. In *Curtin and Labor's Full Employment Promise*, presented to a Curtin University seminar in March 2003, Tim Rowse points out that there was also a Canadian paper on 'Employment and Income' in April 1945 and the Murray-Wagner-Thomas Bill on postwar employment introduced to US Congress in January 1945. Postwar employment policy was 'a preoccupation of the Allies', JCPML00793/1/2.

'the British White Paper': Cornish, pp. 2, 3. J.J. Dedman, the then Minister for Post War Reconstruction, recalled that Curtin had promised a document 'broadly comparable in scope with the British White Paper' when he returned from the Commonwealth Prime Minister's Conference in London in July 1944.

'Ministry of Post War Reconstruction': S. Cornish, *Full Employment in Australia: The Genesis of a White Paper*, p 22.

'Curtin wrote extensive comments': T. Rowse, *Curtin and Labor's Full Employment Promise*, JCPML00793/1/2, devotes eleven pages to analysing Curtin's extensive comments.

'national income going to wages': ibid. Rowse argues the incomes policy issue was left unresolved; that is, if there were full employment, how would inflationary wage increases be contained? This became a more pressing issue by the 1970s.

'There was no significant difference': ibid.

'As Dick Downing . . . recalled': in a review of 'Essays on John Maynard Keynes', *Economic Record*, March 1976, vol. 52. Downing also wrote that 'Australia, thanks to the ideological groundwork of Copland and Giblin . . . and to the statistical application of Keynes's ideas by Colin Clark and Horrie Brown, was well ahead' of England and America in adopting Keynes.

'commitment to full employment': S.J. Butlin and C.B. Schedvin, *The War Economy 1942–1945*, p. 347.

'from February 1942': this section draws heavily on Butlin and Schedvin, ibid., p. 630.

'began to swing the other way': these attitudes on tariffs were not unusual and were widely held by economists. Melville recorded in his oral history that as chairman of the Tariff Board, 'I always acted with the presumption that tariffs were good policy for Australia', that no country had industrialised without them because of infant industry argument, and that it would be decades before Australia was able to take them off.

'believed in February 1943': S.J. Butlin and C.B. Schedvin, *The War Economy 1942–1945*, pp. 633–4.

'Giblin and Coombs agreed': as Butlin concluded, 'in 1942 official economists rejected liberal internationalism as a basis for postwar planning'.

'the highest possible level of demand': S.J. Butlin and C.B. Schedvin, *The War Economy 1942–1945*, p. 632.

'Keynes found the Australians': see D.J. Markwell, *Keynes and Australia*, RBA Discussion Paper, 2002.

'Curtin was markedly more liberal': see his 1 November 1934 speech in the Address-in-Reply, CPD, vol. 145, 1 November 1934, with an extract in D. Black, *In His Own Words*, Paradigm Books, Curtin University, Perth, 1995, p. 123.

'in February 1945': E. Ronald Walker, *The Australian Economy in War and Reconstruction*, Oxford University Press, New York, 1947, pp. 406–7.

'membership of the new institutions': E.G. Whitlam, speech given at the Chifley Memorial Dinner, 7 September 1991, p. 17.

8 Curtin in the Australian Story

'an Australian Settlement': P. Kelly, *The End of Certainty*, Allen
& Unwin, Sydney, 1994, p. 1.

'By the end of the war': S.J. Butlin and C.B. Schedvin, *War
Economy 1942–1945*, Australian War Memorial, Canberra,
1997, p. 347.

'Now Maher joined other young people': JCPML, Records of
James Maher. Anecdotal memory of John Curtin and his
Cabinet, 1995, JCPML00046/1.

'They bothered young Eunice': JCPML, Records of Eunice Lee.
Anecdotal memory of John Curtin and Alexander Thomas
by Eunice Lee, 1996, JCPML00145/1.

Index